Other Women

Between Men ~ Between Women
Lesbian and Gay Studies
Lillian Faderman and Larry Gross, Editors

Other Women

Lesbian / Bisexual Experience and
Psychoanalytic Views of Women

Beverly Burch

Columbia University Press
NEW YORK

Certain chapters of this book are based on prior publications of the author and are used by permission of the publishers. The author gratefully acknowledges permission from the following publishers and journals to reprint previously published material in a revised form. Parts of chapters 1 and 2 used material from "Heterosexuality, Bisexuality, and Lesbianism: Rethinking Psychoanalytic Views of Women's Sexual Object Choice," *Psychoanalytic Review* 80(1):82–99, copyright © National Psychological Association for Psychoanalysis. Chapter 3: "Gender Identities, Lesbianism, and Potential Space," *Psychoanalytic Psychology* 10(3):359–375, copyright © 1993 Lawrence Erlbaum Associates. Reprinted in J. M. Glassgold and S. Iasenza, eds., *Lesbians and Psychoanalysis: Revolutions in Theory and Practice*, copyright © Judith M. Glassgold and Suzanne Iasenza; revised with permission of the Free Press, a division of Simon and Schuster. Chapter 4: "Between Women: The Mother-Daughter Romance and Homoerotic Transference," *Psychoanalytic Psychology* 13(4):475–494, copyright © Lawrence Erlbaum Associates. Chapter 5 uses material from "Psychotherapy and the Dynamics of Merger in Lesbian Couples," in Terry S. Stein and Carol J. Cohen, eds., *Psychotherapy with Gay Men and Lesbians*, copyright © 1986 Plenum Publishing Co., and "Another Perspective on Merger in Lesbian Relationships," in Lynne Bravo Rosewater and Lenore Walker, eds., *Handbook of Feminist Therapy: Women's Issues in Psychotherapy*, copyright © 1985 Springer Publishing Co. Chapter 6 uses material from "Barriers to Intimacy: Conflicts Over Power, Dependency, and Nurturing in Lesbian Relationships," in Boston Lesbian Psychologies Collective, ed., *Lesbian Psychologies*, copyright © 1987 University of Illinois Press. Chapter 7: "Lesbian Sexuality/Female Sexuality: Searching for Subjectivity," *Psychoanalytic Review*, copyright © National Psychological Association for Psychoanalysis.

Columbia University Press
Publishers Since 1893
New York   Chichester, West Sussex
Copyright © 1997 Columbia University Press
All rights reserved

Library of Congress Cataloging-in-Publication Data
Burch, Beverly.
     Other women : lesbian / bisexual experience and psychoanalytic views of women / Beverly Burch.
          p.   cm.
     Includes bibliographical references and index.
     ISBN 0–231–10602–5 (cloth). — ISBN 0–231–10603–3 (pbk.)
     1. Lesbianism—Psychological aspects.   2. Psychoanalysis and feminism.   3. Women and psychoanalysis.   4. Bisexual women— psychology.   5. Psychoanalysis and homosexuality.   I. Title.
RC451.4.G39B87   1997
616.89'17'086643—dc20   96–41400
                                                                CIP

Casebound editions of Columbia University Press books are printed on permanent and durable acid-free paper.

Printed in the United States of America

c 10 9 8 7 6 5 4 3 2 1
p 10 9 8 7 6 5 4 3 2 1

Between Men ~ Between Women
Lesbian and Gay Studies
Lillian Faderman and Larry Gross, Editors

Advisory Board of Editors

Claudia Card
Terry Castle
John D'Emilio
Esther Newton
Anne Peplau
Eugene Rice
Kendall Thomas
Jeffrey Weeks

Between Men ~ Between Women is a forum for current lesbian and gay scholarship in the humanities and social sciences. The series includes both books that rest within specific traditional disciplines and are substantially about gay men, bisexuals, or lesbians and books that are interdisciplinary in ways that reveal new insights into gay, bisexual, or lesbian experience, transform traditional disciplinary methods in consequence of the perspectives that experience provides, or begin to establish lesbian and gay studies as a freestanding inquiry. Established to contribute to an increased understanding of lesbians, bisexuals, and gay men, the series also aims to provide through that understanding a wider comprehension of culture in general.

To Linda O'Brien and Annie O'Brien Burch

Contents

Preface

Other Women: Lesbian/Bisexual Experience and Psychoanalytic Views of Women is an effort to create something of what I have found missing as a therapist and a feminist: an understanding of women in general and lesbians in particular that bridges feminist thinking, psychoanalytic theory, social constructivist views, and clinical experience (which sometimes defies the insights of all of these). In the early 1970s, when I began training, being a psychotherapist coincided with being a feminist. Feminist psychotherapy was an outgrowth of feminist politics, and the two seemed to be natural allies—congruent, mutually supportive and illuminating. The further I went in practice and in training, however, the more they began to diverge uncomfortably. With some of my friends and colleagues I discovered that a feminist understanding of women may be necessary to psychotherapy, but it is not sufficient.

As feminists and therapists we read together and talked together, broadening our perspective, but we also observed within ourselves and each other the unyielding, the seemingly immutable, irrational constructions and constrictions of self, and struggled with how to reach deeper. Consciousness raising, the primary method of feminism, can be an intrusion in psychotherapy, hindering deeper work. Women in psychotherapy are already generally too concerned with whether their thoughts, feelings, dreams, fantasies, and behavior are "appropriate," "correct," "healthy," or acceptable.

Traditional psychotherapy has been problematic for feminism. Humanist psychology, which more or less embraces feminism, devalues depth psychology, but its own limits are evident when psychotherapy continues beyond brief therapy. As a result, I was more and more drawn to that which feminism identified as the adversary: psychoanalytic theory. Psychoanalytic theory has traditionally been impervious to feminist thought (or much of any thought outside of its own internal debates). Periodically, I would attend a psychoanalytic conference that was ostensibly concerned with a more progressive view of women (forget lesbians), only to be very disappointed. I would abandon hope, temporarily, of any meaningful integration of the two. When Nancy Chodorow's and Dorothy Dinnerstein's work appeared, it was heartening. They provided a conceptual breakthrough for many of us. Gradually the irresistible force of feminism seemed to be meeting the immovable object of psychoanalysis.

I studied psychoanalytic theory with a few eminent analysts, outside of training institutes (which in those days would have been unlikely to admit me anyway). I attended lectures, went to analytic therapy, read the literature, and found other women with similar interests. I began writing about lesbians in the early 1980s, when it still seemed risky to apply psychoanalytic ideas to lesbian relationships. I anticipated objections from lesbian readers and disregard by psychoanalysts. Both expectations were met, but I also had many positive responses. All of these reactions continue to some degree, but now there are many lesbians (clinicians, academics) interested in psychoanalytic/psychodynamic thinking and there are some psychoanalysts interested in lesbian psychology beyond what has been almost a party line concerning the pathology of homosexuality.

Elsewhere, within academia, feminist and psychoanalytic thinking have been incorporated into many disciplines, and academic readers are generally more interested in bridging the two theories. There, however, other boundaries are treacherous. The ascendance of postmodernism in the university has meant that social constructivism replaced anything approximating essentialist thought. Many of the biases of the culture at large and specifically of psychoanalysis have been (happily) cast into disrepute there. Nevertheless, an inclusive rather than exclusive orientation is appealing to me, and I cannot altogether abandon certain ideas and constructs (the Self, for example). The limitations and biases of essentialist thinking do have their counterparts in social constructionism, and a balancing act is sometimes necessary between them.

Accepting, at least temporarily, a limited concept may be the only way to proceed. This has certainly been true for me with psychoanalysis. Possibilities inherent in biogenetic and ethnobiological interpretations of human experience—again essentialist—are intriguing. These ideas are not impossibly at odds with either a constructivist or a psychoanalytic understanding, although they require a continuing process of rethinking and reintegrating. Psychoanalysis still greatly values mythology and metaphor, while at the other extreme academic psychology tends to discount anything that cannot be quantified. Borrowing from different methodologies—crossing back and forth between empirical perspectives, clinical observations, and sometimes antithetical theoretical analyses—is like translating English into other, very different, languages without relying on paraphrasing too often.

Not being officially affiliated with psychoanalytic or academic institutions is in some ways a fortunate position to be in. I do not have to worry about professional consequences of incorrect thinking, nor am I overly influenced (I hope) by ideological positions. In any case, the atmosphere in which I have lived and written has changed enormously, and even psychoanalytic institutions show progress. A number of important psychoanalytic books and papers are being written about gay and lesbian experience and psychology, and presumably they are sometimes read within these institutions as well.

Other Women brings together papers published in feminist and psychoanalytic journals from the early 1980s up to the present as well as some new writing. Over the years it has been satisfying to return to the perceptions first articulated by feminism, only now with an enriched understanding, appreciating the role of unconscious processes and the development of "deep" psychological structures. Most of the papers in this book are relatively new ones, and the early papers have been revised and elaborated upon. All of them challenge some prevailing psychoanalytic notions, but they have largely been published in psychoanalytic journals, verifying that changes are taking place. There is much other work available now—mostly from other women (i.e., Other Women)—and their ideas have been very helpful and stimulating. A real cross-fertilization of feminist psychoanalytic thinking about lesbianism and homosexuality is beginning to be possible.

I have tried to maintain an awareness of cultural issues beyond what some of the earlier papers possessed. For example, as often as possible the race or ethnicity or geographical background and age of individual women whom I quoted or described are identified. No implications are drawn from these identifications. Too few individuals are quoted or described in this book to make any interpretations of cultural experience, which are complex in any case. Omitting these identifications, however, promotes false assumptions of homogeneity among lesbians, quite the opposite of what I want to convey. Simply noting these identities makes it clear that a diverse group of women have a diverse group of experiences under the broad category of "lesbian."

The first part of the book is primarily concerned with individual issues: gender identity, developing sexual preference, erotic/romantic dynamics within family life. The second part is about experiences within families women create for themselves—with each other, with or without children. The theme of lesbian, bisexual, and certain heterosexual women as Other runs through the book, each chapter elaborating on it in its own way. Various other themes are treated from different perspectives in different chapters. For example, the myth of Demeter and Persephone recurs throughout the book, but with a slightly different cast to the story each time. The family romance is also a prevailing metaphor, and the vicissitudes of love between mothers and daughters is of special interest. Chapter 4 takes the daughter's perspective in the heterosexual family, while chapter 8 takes the mothers' perspective in the lesbian family. This is not a linear narrative. The chapters do not need to be read in the order they appear for connecting links to emerge. The larger perspective is clear, I hope, in whatever way each reader might approach the book.

Acknowledgments

I would like to thank all those who influenced me over the years of writing these essays and this book. That list would include teachers, supervisors, therapists, clients, friends, family, and writing colleagues, spanning almost my whole professional career as a psychotherapist—twenty years' worth. Often I don't know exactly when ideas began and how they were expanded and enriched by others. I know that I am grateful to have spent these twenty years in the Bay Area, a community of many talented and independent-minded psychotherapists who have provided an intellectual atmosphere I needed. I thanked many of them in my earlier book, and I won't repeat the list here, but their support continues to be vital to me.

A number of people gave me specific help with turning these essays into a book. I am grateful to Sheryl Fullerton and Lillian Faderman, who helped me get the manuscript into the right hands, to Margaret Buttenheim, who critiqued and championed it, and to Judy Eron who proofread it for me at a difficult time. My editor, Ann Miller, has been enthusiastic and supportive from beginning to end, always making herself available when I needed something. Susan Pensak's careful reading and thoughtful suggestions allowed me to relax about whether it was ready.

I am very grateful to Linda (Heine) O'Brien, who has been in my life all these years, putting up with the hours I spent at the computer.

She quietly placed a four-inch Buddha, drinking coffee and talking on the phone, on top of the computer so that, whenever I was struggling, I could meditate on the folly of what I was doing. She supported, encouraged, criticized, and sustained me and then carried on. When our four-year-old daughter, Annie, put her little plastic Pooh bear on top of the computer next to the Buddha, I knew it was time to finish. I am thankful to be constantly inspired by her.

Other Women

Introduction: Other Women

O *ther Women* is about women who are Other, that is, women who do not identify with the traditional feminine images of this culture. Women who are not heterosexual and/or women who do not fit the traditional sense of what is feminine are Other. They do not find their own reflection when they look into the cultural mirror of women's lives: they aren't represented in the mainstream media, and their place in psychological discourse is one of deviance or pathology.

Many, perhaps most, women feel a sense of otherness: men are the norm, women are other. How much more alien, then, is the sensibility of women who experience yet another degree of differentiation from the norm. In one way or another perhaps all women know that aspects of their inner lives do not fit traditional gender or sexual norms. For some women, however, this alienation is fundamental. They know themselves to be Other.

Otherness is a matter of categories—humanly created divisions and decisions about where to draw the lines. Norms are established and what is and what is not to be recognized is sanctioned. Otherness is primarily a matter of subjectivity vs. objectivity. Are you the one asking the questions or the one about whom the questions are asked— the observer or the observed? When you are asking the questions, you can draw the lines, you can reposition everyone. Instead of placing traditional heterosexual women in the center and looking at lesbian, bisexual, and nontraditional women out there on the periphery, I place these other women in the center of the story.

Whoever stands in the center determines the perspective. People adopt other people's perspectives, perspectives that don't match their own experience very well, and substitute them for their own, particularly when those other views are the sanctioned ones. In this way racial minorities incorporate a sense of inferiority and women come to believe they are (or should be) whatever men say they are or want them to be. All are limited in this way: deeply held beliefs, sometimes not even conscious, make it extremely difficult to think beyond the received cultural perspective.

To understand women we rely upon theories that are not very appealing. The nuclear family is apparently the developmental training ground, and it offers the prototypes for heterosexuality and femininity. The standard version is that girls fall in love with fathers and identify with mothers. They grow up to choose men who remind them in some way of their fathers and they keep on struggling to be like or unlike their mothers. Why does it happen this way? Usually this version of female development is simply treated as inevitable, even as biology.

Man and woman together, definitively masculine and feminine, *must* be a prototype, *must* be what is natural and normal. Even ethologists, who study animal behavior, rarely study homosexuality in animals, although it is even more common than in humans and occurs in diverse circumstances (Fisher 1992). Why isn't homosexuality in animals studied more? Is it considered to be less interesting or less significant? Apparently ethologists' attitudes and observations are influenced by cultural dictates. The prevalence of animal homosexuality easily challenges cultural ideas about the unnaturalness of sexual variation. The view of heterosexuality and dichotomous gender identity as biologically ordained has been deeply accepted; even theorists who attempt to think about sexuality and identity in other terms—Freud, for example—do not get very far.

Freud tried to rewrite the story of sexuality, enough to place bisexuality at the center of what is essential to human sexuality. He too could not think past the givens of his (our) culture, which equated desiring women with being masculine and desiring men with being feminine. He could imagine universal bisexuality, but his bisexuality was based on the prototype. To Freud, bisexuality involved a shift in identity: one's gender shifted along with one's desires. If one loved/desired a woman, one was feeling like a man, regardless. He could not imagine sexual desire as independent of gender. Further, he could not think of gender itself as something other than innate, essential—or, again, normal and natural. Masculinity and femininity, as defined in the culture, were meant to be.

In his first essay about sexuality Freud (1905) referred to a passage in Plato's *Symposium* in which Aristophanes explains the nature of sexual attraction.[1] Aristophanes tells his story about how the earliest human beings, our primordial ancestors, were cut in half by the gods and then forever devoted themselves to searching for their other half. Freud writes:

> The popular theory of the sexual instinct corresponds closely to the poetic fable of dividing the person into two halves—man and woman who strive to become reunited through love. It is, therefore, very surprising to find that there are men for whom the sexual object is not woman but man, and that there are women for whom it is not man but woman. (1905:146)

But Freud's recollection of this myth is inaccurate. Aristophanes' tale in *The Symposium* actually begins this way: "In the first place the sexes were originally three in number, not two as they are now; there was man, woman, and the union of the two, having a name corresponding to this double nature" (Jowett 1933:315). All three types of beings were divided in half, and each of them continued to seek their other half. Aristophanes has a low opinion of the men and women who come from the androgynous beings, i.e., the heterosexual ones; according to him they are lascivious and adulterous. Women who were once part of the original woman are only interested in other women and men who were once the original man continue to seek other men. Aristophanes says these men "have the most manly nature."

In this narrative lesbians are quintessentially female and homosexual men quintessentially male. Heterosexuals are the androgynous beings. Somehow, to Freud, this myth served as a template for heterosexuality. His distorted recollection of the story embodies the biases inherent in modern thinking about human sexuality and love, which treats homosexuality as a gender problem. (It also ignores Aristophanes' bias that heterosexuals are the problematic ones.) Recognizing Freud's use of the myth reminds us how entrenched we all are in contemporary ways of thinking about sexuality and gender. Thinking of male and female as the only complements to each other is heterocentric (and heterosexist) thinking.

In trying to alter the story of sexual development from a biological one to a psychological one, Freud depicts the daughter as so wounded by her own sense of inferiority in being female that she shifts her love from her mother to her father. She feels injured and outraged because she doesn't have a penis; she blames her mother and is irremediably disappointed in her. Because her mother also lacks a penis, she too is devalued, and the father is the only truly desirable one. The poor daughter hopes to make up for her own lack by winning the father's love and later by having a baby (symbolically the father's baby). Thus her heterosexuality is founded on her own misogyny, her own dislike and disparagement of being female. She is stuck with being a woman, but at least she can lay claim to a man. How, then, could we understand the depth of women's ties to each other?

If the person to write the first psychodynamic narrative of family sexuality had been a woman, the story would surely have had a different bias.

The psychoanalytic narrative of lesbian development is even worse, of course, and is a story that keeps changing. Contradictory versions have attributed it variously to fixation on the mother, some congenital factor, or failure to resolve a "masculinity" complex (i.e., a lesbian never gives up on having her own penis). Freud couldn't seem to decide whether homosexuality was pathological or not; he also wavered about how much lesbianism had to do with female masculinity—a curious oxymoron.

Another problem with the psychoanalytic narrative: if sexuality is psychodynamically fixed by the family in early years, how do we account for women who begin their adult sexual lives interested in relationships with men but eventually move to relationships with women? Many of these women come to identify as lesbian without renouncing their early or continuing interest in men. What about women who have lovers of both sexes or who don't choose partners according to sex but according to other criteria? Bisexuality in adult years is not accounted for anywhere. Is it somehow a matter of these women growing up with innate bisexuality intact (cf. Morton 1993)?

For Freud, and the mainstream of twentieth-century Western culture, anatomical sex, gender, sexual choices, and biology might as well all be treated as different facets of the same thing. This easy congruency seems to make sense, at least on the surface, to those who grow up with these assumptions entrenched in their culture. Deviations occur, true, but they can be treated as errors. Apparently even nature makes errors.

What if one grows up in a very different culture, however? The picture will surely not look the same. If the family constitution is not nuclear, and biological fathers don't belong to the core family group; if the mother's brothers and male cousins take more care and interest in her children than the biological father does; if biological mothers don't raise their children exclusively or necessarily, but share this role with other women in their family or community; if being adopted and raised by other adults in the community is common—then the communal story of family life and erotic alliances will surely be quite different. If one grows up in a culture that defines gender in terms of three of four categories, not two; if almost everyone in the community has homosexual experiences at some point in their lives; if homosexual marriages are sanctioned, even privileged; if homosexual "affairs" are presumed to coexist with marriage, sometimes challenging the pleasure or legitimacy of the other, sometimes not—then again sexual and gender choices will be framed in ways contrary to our own.

There are cultures throughout the world and throughout history that are or once were characterized by one or all of these communal and familial structures.² Has anyone ever asked people from such different cultures what our picture of normal development looks like to them? I do not know, but I imagine that if one came from such a culture our view would look not particularly normal but strangely contrived. The expressions of sexuality and gender in our culture would probably not seem to be innate or even especially appealing.

Women's Value to Each Other

Women have always had primary relationships with each other: as friends, lovers, sisters, as mothers and daughters. It is not rare, I think, for a woman to feel that one of these relationships has been the key relationship of her life. This importance may seem obvious for women who are lesbian, whose intimate lives center around other women. Yet others, heterosexual and bisexual women, also often hold a relationship with a particular woman in a place of special significance, matching or surpassing the significance of relationships with husbands or lovers.

We find these relationships in narrative literature: Jane Austen's *Pride and Prejudice* and *Sense and Sensibility*, Virginia Woolf's *To The Lighthouse*, Doris Lessing's *The Golden Notebook*, Toni Morrison's *Sula*, Tillie Olsen's stories in *Tell Me A Riddle* became the novels of the women's movement because they articulate the loyalty, heartache, or longing of women for each other—sisters, friends, mothers, and daughters. When women in these novels suffer, the wound comes from feelings for another woman, not a man. In the 1970s recognition of the centrality of women to each others' lives began to grow. This, I believe, as much as political commitment, drew women into the movement. Suddenly there was a shared awareness of something women had not even articulated individually.

Why was it so necessary and so liberating to find that other women felt such longing and such vulnerability? The question of women's vulnerability vis-à-vis each other is one of the concerns of this book. The women's movement shifted its focus, at least in the public arena of feminism, to economic disparities, individual development, and the threats to women's physical safety; the emotional sparks that reignited feminism thirty years ago are no longer so apparent. I wonder if young women are having to rediscover these things for themselves, and I wonder if it is still so difficult.

Women have in some sense always known how important they are to each other and have not always needed to talk about it. Except for unfriendly metaphors ("fighting like cats," "two old biddies,"), however, women's relationships with each other have limited means of representation in ordinary discourse. *Sisters* has been the primary signifier of women's loyalty or love for each other, and the dynamics of sisterhood have not even been looked at very often. Instead it stands as an idealized relationship, unexamined in its risks, failures, and complexities. Women's relationships with each other, with the exception of mother-daughter relationships, lack elaboration. Even in mother-daughter relationships a significant dimension has been neglected: the love affair that begins at birth and often falls under the shadow of its counterpart—what our culture seizes upon for mothers and sons—the so-called oedipal relationship.

Perhaps relationships between women are different from relationships between women and men. If so, we learn something different about women by observing their relationships with each other than we do by observing their relationships with men or by observing women individually. We can question the received wisdom, psychodynamic and sociological, about women and women's relationships. Looking at lesbian relationships as a kind of template is useful, not only to lesbians but to other women as well. Naive heterosexuals, pondering lesbians, ask, What do women do with each other? meaning, What do women do sexually? It's an interesting question, really, and the answer less obvious than one might think. If we ask the same question referring to what women do emotionally and psychologically as well, the answer may also be complicated.

The essays in this book about women and relationships—lesbian, bisexual, heterosexual women and their various relationships with each other—attempt to move the cultural discourse along in its awareness and representation of diverse women's lives. They are concerned with both sexuality and gender, with differences between expressions of sexuality, with femininity or masculinity as multiplicities, with the consequences of cultural choices for the individual, with difficulties women feel in being sexual at all. These essays question the fundamental divisions between women. Is there really something internal that distinguishes lesbian women from heterosexual, or both from bisexual? Are these categories real, or are they social constructions with some limited use? They have been reified in much of psychological and social theory and research; perhaps they simply do more harm than good.

Elsewhere, I have made a distinction between primary and bisexual lesbians, discarding the notion that homosexuality (male or female) is monolithic and that all lesbians share a similar psychology or developmental history (Burch 1992). I have also suggested that sexuality can be thought of as a continuum from primary lesbian to primary heterosexual—those women whose desires and interests seem to be focused exclusively on other women or men. In between are bisexual lesbians, bisexuals (who don't identify as either lesbian or heterosexual), and what might be called bisexual heterosexuals. Even these distinctions are arbitrary, although sometimes useful theoretically.

People are not alike, and distinctions can be meaningful. But these distinctions are not fixed ones, not innately determined (even if biologically or genetically influenced). Homosexuality and heterosexuality are behaviors, not conditions. Homosexual or heterosexual identity is a subjective sense of self that may alter, one way or another, like femininity or masculinity. These identities are influenced by both time and place. Before the nineteenth-century designation of homosexuality as a condition and a kind of person or even personality, no one considered himself or herself to be such, regardless of sexual desires. In other cultures today this kind of identity fixing is alien, even though same-sex desires and relationships are familiar. Nevertheless, throughout this book I often refer to lesbians, bisexuals, and heterosexuals in the usual way, as if these are categories that correspond to reality. The existence of these categories has created their reality. At the same time I also continue to discuss and discard these sexual and gender categories.

When people assume that lesbians and heterosexual women are fundamentally different, they may point to these differences to try to identify what's wrong with lesbians. The similarities are equally informative. For example, I keep observing what we learn about women in general from lesbian relationships, things that aren't so apparent if one is looking at women alone or in relationships with men. Again, so much depends upon one's point of view. If one assumes lesbian behavior to be problematic, or lesbian identity to be pathological, one treats differences as diagnostic. If one does not make that assumption, differences have another function: they point to the unseen potential in women's development.

Likewise with gender differences: if one stops using a polarized view of human characteristics—masculine vs. feminine—women who do not fit the feminine prototype inform us about a broader range of women's potential rather than about "masculinity" in women. The heterosexual Other women are nontraditional in at least one of two— again oxymoronic—ways: they are "masculine women" and/or they are "bisexual heterosexuals." They too differ from the feminine prototype in some significant way. By bisexual I mean women who form relationships with other women that are primary or central to their lives even though they are heterosexual. They may be married, they may prefer sex with men, they may be afraid of or never have considered sex with women, but their deepest emotional ties manifest themselves bisexually: their love of other women (or of one other woman) matches or surpasses their love of a man.

While using psychoanalytic thinking and certain psychodynamic premises, such as unconscious desires, self-representations, and internalized relationships, as a way of looking beyond the surfaces of behavior and expressed feeling, one can also challenge psychoanalytic and other cultural assumptions that claim special knowledge of what is natural, or given by nature, and what is healthy. Feminism and postmodernism attempt to send such traditional beliefs back to their owners, asking us to understand that what is observed is determined by the convictions of the observer, conscious or otherwise.

We are capable of holding onto many threads of thought even while we are working with one or two. It is possible to use intuitive knowledge, communal wisdom, and interpretive reading of experience as well as scientific methodology and empirical data, maintaining awareness of their relative contributions and lapses. Scientific theories and research about biological processes (sociobiology, for example) are important, but how could one think they are sufficient for understanding the complexities of human sexuality, profoundly shaped as it is by family dynamics and cultural construction? Likewise, to think of human sexuality as culturally constructed, solely created by time and place (social psychology) denies our animal existence. There may well be some biological givens in sexuality and gender, even if we cannot isolate them.

The problem again is with the categories themselves. Creating dichotomies—biology vs. psychology, heterosexuality vs. homosexuality, masculinity vs. femininity—sets their constituents up to do battle. It is endemic in our culture to make polarities and treat them as antagonistic.

These essays draw from many sources, professional, personal, and scholarly. Some use clinical insights with women in psychotherapy, some employ informal interviews and conversations with women, some refer to empirical research, some are based on theoretical material by other writers.[3] In thinking about women's development, I start with the family romance, the love between family members that is so quickly complicated by other emotions and needs. We already have a narrative about the "correct" family romance, but what about the other versions? I keep returning to the family romance because it stays with us in one way or another throughout our lives, whether we re-create it or react against it. Even grown up, with adult relationships or families of our own, we are likely to keep playing off of that old tune, forever reworking it.

Using other perspectives, such as feminism and postmodernism, one tries to keep account of cultural, epistomological biases. Still stretching one's perceptions of what is normal, one is nevertheless bound by one's own cultural givens. Other perspectives render old pictures obsolete, but they are themselves reminders of our limitations, of the fact that anyone can only use whatever she is given as a way of seeing a little more or a little differently. Humbled, we have to give up the idea that there will finally be a correct picture or a complete picture.

PART ONE

*Psychoanalytic Theory and
Narratives of Women*

The Mythology of the Family Romance

When describing gender and sexual development and psychological structure, both psychoanalytic and Jungian theories use Greek mythology as if they were expressions of universal truth. Both theories selectively use tales of heterosexual love and neglect the homoerotic narratives, perpetuating the myth of our time that heterosexuality is the essential feature of human sexuality and gender. Essentialist beliefs function as a barrier to critical thinking, especially about the diversity of sexual and gender expression. Mythopoetic traditions still compel interest, but their place in theory deserves more analysis—their use is perhaps more revealing of theorists' desires and motivations than it is of "human nature." This is particularly true of the Oedipus story, which has come to be viewed as a fact of human development.

Freud's primary concern was with the period in early development when family relationships become triangulated. The child is caught in a love triangle with father and mother and has to manage all the desire, jealousy, and competition this arouses. Freud thought the story of Oedipus aptly expressed the unconscious side of this family drama. He selected the parts of the story that suited this purpose, narrowing it down to what he felt was its core insight: the son wants to get rid of the father so he can have the mother for himself. His omissions matter in that they illuminate his concerns and his method (cf. Balmary 1982).

Freud's version omits the beginning of the narrative: Laius, Oedipus's father, was also taken in and raised by another father, Labdacus. Laius fell in love with Labdacus's son, Chrysippus, and eloped with him. For stealing the king's son, his own house was cursed—his own son would kill him. The first part of the story then is about a different triangle and a different kind of desire: young love, sibling love, homoerotic love, betrayal of the father—a rich story in itself, open to other interpretations about the family. This much more complicated version of the family romance (still primarily about the bonds and rivalries between men) perhaps made little sense to Freud, who had already fixed his idea of what the core family story was. The complexity of the original story—one of multidetermined family dynamics with variations on the nature of sexual desire—suggests that a simple one will not do, at least not as a universal template.

Freud's story—the child's undeniable desires for mother and murderous wishes toward father—establishes oedipal experience universally, across gender and culture. His view was continued with fervor by his followers and the "oedipal period" became entrenched as a fact of early development, the determinant of heterosexuality. The "primacy of the phallus" was how Freud (1923) characterized the entire early developmental period. Aside from the question of how adequate the oedipal story is for male development, it is clearly a male story. Oedipus's story is of struggle between fathers and sons. There is no story for a daughter here.

The themes of the Freudian Oedipus story—lust and competition—concern power as much as erotic desire: he wants to defeat the king (and become king himself) as much as he wants to claim the queen. By killing the father, he satisfies both desires. In psychoanalytic terms, the son desires the mother and the power of the father's penis (the phallus really: not simply the penis itself, but all it represents and endows). He is thrown into risky competition with the father, but once he realizes just how risky it is—his father might take away his penis, he could lose his claim to future power and future women—he retreats. He does not kill his father, but he has fantasized killing him. Thereafter he is vulnerable to guilt and castration anxiety. The pursuit of success becomes a lifetime quest, always accompanied by the anxiety that he will in effect kill his father if he wins or lose the phallus if he fails.

Still using the myth of Oedipus, traditional analytic theory writes the story of female development as if girls were little more than female boys, doomed to imitation and inadequacy. Defined by the norm of a male body—a penis—their genitals are known only by what they lack, not by what they possess. Their story in the family is written as the obverse of the boy's, having no name of its own, but called "the female Oedipus complex." (The *Electra complex* was proposed by Jung; it gained some popular currency, but only slight credit within psychoanalysis. That myth parallels Oedipus's story only in that the daughter aids in the murder of her mother. But the brother is the actual murderer—even here the girl is not the central character of her own story. Further, her passion is for vengeance—their mother has killed their father—not for love or power.)

From its patriarchal vantage point, classical psychoanalytic theory has little choice but to cast female development in a pathological light. Certainly lesbian or bisexual development is problematic—how can there be a happy ending if there's not a happy heterosexual couple at the close of the story? But heterosexual development has an unhappy ending for girls as well. The story of female heterosexuality describes a girl who is narcissistically wounded by her lack of a penis, a wound that can be assuaged but, of course, never repaired. Her wound is so great she loses interest in her own sexual anatomy—it is obviously inferior—and gives up masturbation and clitoral pleasures. The best she can do is possess a penis vicariously by possessing a man. Such a story was impossible even for many of Freud's contemporary female—and some male—analysts to endorse, and feminists have criticized it for decades.

Many current psychoanalytic writers have also addressed the inadequacy of this account, including most recently Thomas Ogden (1987) and Nancy Chodorow (1994). Theoretical contortions are required to account for why the girl abandons her love for her mother in favor of her father: she must resent the mother and turn against her for having made her female, i.e., without a penis, and for being female herself, yet somehow she must still identify with her and wish to be like her. She negates her own anatomy and sexual pleasure, "renouncing" her clitoris. She suppresses her so-called masculinity (active and aggressive desires) and accepts a degree of masochism and misogyny. This, according to Freud (1925 and 1931), is normal development. Even though many theorists have rejected this account, an adequate conception of the complexities of women's sexuality is still lacking.

What is referred to as the preoedipal period of early childhood, the time when the child is preoccupied with mother and supposedly not much concerned with father, is an early love affair in which child and mother are the central characters.[1] The primary issue for the child is the problem of differentiating self from mother while still claiming a primary bond with her, not concern with third parties. Freud, prompted by the work of contemporary female colleagues, began to recognize the saliency of this period for girls in particular and to acknowledge that perhaps the girl did not turn against her mother so thoroughly as he once thought. As many theorists have pointed out, the girl's passage through this period involves only a partial or fluctuating separation from the mother (Deutsch 1944; Chodorow 1978).

The usual starting point for understanding lesbian development has been to determine how it deviates from the supposedly normal path of female sexual development. These deviations are treated as pathological—in spite of ample empirical evidence that lesbians have neither more nor less psychological and emotional difficulties than heterosexual women do.[2] Another problem in traditional theory is the failure to account for the lifelong bisexual orientation that characterizes some women's sexuality.

Freud's diverse and contradictory accounts of lesbian development—fixation on the mother, congenital factors, narcissism, a masculinity complex, etc.—reflect his admitted confusion about women in general. Not only could he not decide whether being a woman was inherently problematic, he could not make up his mind about whether homosexuality was pathological (cf. Lewes 1988). Perhaps it was or perhaps it was simply a variation in the sexual instinct and could be considered abnormal only in a statistical sense. Unfortunately his followers had less personal and theoretical doubt.

The biases of psychoanalysis and the lack of evidence to support analytic theories of lesbian development have been criticized by other disciplines and by empirical researchers. A review of the psychoanalytic literature on lesbian psychodynamics finds these variables responsible for lesbian object choice: father-daughter relationships that are difficult, father-daughter relationships that are especially close, mother-daughter relationships that are distant, mother-daughter relationships that are overly close, and poor relationships with both parents. Certainly all the bases are covered. Empirical studies have not found any significant differences in the family relationships of heterosexual and homosexual women however (Shavelson et al. 1980).

More Theoretical Mythology

The Oedipus story may not describe universal male developmental issues as it purports to, but its themes are characteristically male ones. The oedipal myth would be adequate in depicting female development only if one persisted in overlooking the obvious discrepancies. The girl's early concerns seem less a pursuit of power and more a pursuit of relationships. She does not necessarily compete with her mother so much as she tries to hold onto her while she embraces (so to speak) the father. The daughter's interest in her father does not necessarily eclipse her interest in her mother. She wants both. Why not? The myth of Demeter and Persephone more aptly describes the daughter's developmental crisis.

In this myth the mother-daughter relationship exists first unto itself, without intrusion by the father or the world of men. Demeter as goddess of crops and Persephone as goddess of the spring are companions in innocence and joy until Persephone is lured away from her mother's side to look at a beautiful flower, then abducted and raped by Hades. Persephone lives in the underworld until her mother finds her and achieves her release. Before she returns to her mother, however, Persephone eats six pomegranate seeds in Hades, half knowing, half unaware that this act will require her to return to the underworld six months of each year.

The story describes how the male's entry into the story ends the exclusive nature of the mother–daughter bond; henceforth the daughter's existence moves back and forth between mother and (symbolic) father. Her dilemma is that of a divided psyche, oscillating between two worlds. Note that Persephone wanders off on her own—she separates herself to a degree from her mother—before the father can enter. Some accounts of the myth emphasize the daughter's sorrow at separation from the mother, while others point out her complicity in it (Hertzberg 1962; Hamilton 1969). Both versions are necessary, expressing the daughter's wish to separate and also her wish to keep her exclusive relationship with the mother. In wandering off alone and in eating the pomegranate seeds, she plays her part. Like Oedipus, she is not fully aware of the implications of her deeds.

A subtheme in the myth is that of rape, implying that there is danger for the daughter in relation to the male. Demeter, the mother, is unable to protect her daughter. Both are lost in grief for months until Demeter finally secures the intervention of Zeus. Rhea, the mother of the gods, helps to restore Demeter's daughter to her for part of the year and remains to comfort her for the remainder of the year. This aspect of the story suggests what can happen to girls and women in relation to men—that their integrity or wholeness is at risk. Just as classical Freudians see women's anatomy and psychology as inferior to the male's and likewise see less potential in women, the cultural view of sexual differences also limits women's potential, especially within heterosexuality. Many of the major and more powerful goddesses avoid relationships with men. The meaning of this mythopoetic theme has not been explored psychoanalytically.

Persephone was not one of these singular goddesses however. A footnote to Persephone's story is that she later claims a young man of her own, Adonis. Aphrodite hides Adonis away with Persephone in the underworld when he is a baby; he is so beautiful she doesn't want anyone else to see him. She returns to reclaim him when he is grown, but Persephone has fallen in love with him and won't give him up. Zeus intervenes and gives him to each for half the year. Persephone has Adonis with her in Hades in autumn and winter and returns him to Aphrodite when she rejoins her mother in the world in spring and summer. She thus chooses a lover for herself but still continues her time with Demeter.

The Myth of Universality

Feminist psychoanalytic thinkers, especially Lacanians, attempt to understand the oedipal story in ways that include women, addressing cultural givens instead of biological ones. Here the "lack" that women experience is culturally determined through the culture (language) of patriarchy, not through nature. Women may possess the phallus (as signifier of authority and authoritativeness, not as the penis) through their own agency, with the aid of parental identifications. I question why we need to struggle with a distorting schematic representation of female sexuality and development instead of abandoning it. When the girl is placed in the center of the story, the story itself alters.

Theory needs to provide understanding of early development as the child shifts from a dyadic, rather undifferentiated, bond with a mothering person to a complicated family dynamic involving three— or more. The threesome may be configured in a number of ways, with the participants sometimes playing various parts, as I will discuss later. The narrative of Demeter and Persephone improves on the story of Oedipus as a prototype for female development. It is a representation, missing in psychoanalytic theory, of intense love between mothers and daughters, of grief attending their separation, and of their continuing bond after the advent of the father. It even suggests the continuing challenges in female adult development: Demeter must learn to let go of her daughter periodically. Her own well-being requires that she tolerate greater separation without letting go altogether.

Christine Downing argues that the Demeter-Persephone story also signifies lesbian love, with its characteristic struggle between merger and differentiation (which I will discuss in chapter 5). She writes that

Demeter reminds us of a time when there were no boundaries, when lover and beloved were one. I believe that all close bonds between women inevitably conjure up memories and feelings associated with our first connection to a woman. . . . The pull to reexperience that bond of fusion, that sense of being totally loved, totally known, totally one with another—and the fear of reexperiencing that bond of fusion, of being swallowed up by a relationship, of losing one's own hard-won identity—enter powerfully into all woman–woman relationships. (1989:204)

The Demeter-Persephone narrative invites us to question whether female development is qualitatively different from male development. Rather than the inherently hostile same-sex relationship of the Oedipus story, it shifts the emphasis to the task of managing complex relationships—how to continue in relationship with more than one loved person without losing the self. Will alternation work?

Perhaps more than the boy, the girl holds onto all her loved ones (love objects, in psychoanalytic terms), desiring both, wanting to identify with both. For her, mastery is existing within a three-party relationship without losing anyone, including herself. Competition is a part, but only a part, of this struggle. Perhaps it is the signifier of this time only when all the parties—parents as well as child—have been unable to master their respective developmental tasks. If all does go well, the daughter learns to manage complex relationships, developing the expertise in relationships that many women do seem to have.

But is the story of Demeter and Persephone any more universal for girls than Oedipus is for boys? Why, for example, does psychoanalysis ignore the mythic stories of gods and goddesses, heroes and heroines who are not interested in heterosexuality or who are not defined by sexuality at all? Downing (1989) notes that, except for Ares and Hades, all the major gods have some erotic involvement with men. (Surely some of these tales are more relevant to development for some males than the story of Oedipus.) Goddesses, however, are usually depicted as asexual if they are not interested in men. Many of these stories exist about women—Hestia, Atalanta, Artemis, Athena, to name a few.

Artemis, for example, prefers the company of nymphs, but this is not a love story. Is this asexuality a consequence of the Greek stories having been authored by male poets and playwrights? Does it address the contradiction between full female development and heterosexuality within patriarchal culture?

Downing points out that Athena, who sprang from the head of her father and knows no mother, carries both male and female insignia; she reminds us that so-called masculine qualities are feminine attributes here. She suggests that contemporary "butch" women are represented by Athena. Athena's heritage is often forgotten: her mother, Metis, was impregnated by Zeus. Metis told Zeus that her child would be greater than he, so Zeus swallowed her up whole to prevent the birth. Athena was born anyway, however, full-grown from Zeus's head. Is this not the family story of some girls?

Chodorow (1994) remarks that Freud's description of "non-feminine" development, the girl who identifies with her father instead of desiring him and thus forecloses her own sexuality, corresponds to the story of Athena. She may leave her sexuality unresolved, or perhaps only her heterosexuality. Freud's daughter Anna was, as he recognized, one of these contemporary Athenas, and she spent her life with another woman (Gay 1988). Whether they were lovers or not, we do not know.[3] This relationship was certainly lesbian in an emotional sense, however, if not a sexual one—they created several homes together, traveled together, raised children together. It exemplified the Boston marriage, the apparently asexual relationship between women prevalent in the nineteenth and early twentieth centuries, which enjoyed social approval and even high status among intellectuals of that era.[4]

There are also narratives of cruelty and abandonment in mother-daughter relationships. Iphigenia's mother Clytemnestra was tricked into allowing Agamemnon the father to take her away to sacrifice her (so that he could win the Trojan war). Is that not another parable of family life, the mother who cannot or does not interfere to save the daughter from the father? In another story Aphrodite's jealousy of Psyche's beauty and of her own son Cupid's infatuation with Psyche leads her to place a curse on her. Like European fairy tales,

the mother who curses the daughter apparently must be the step-
mother or mother-in-law. And, there is again the story of Electra, the
daughter who sides with her father and feels murderous rage toward
her mother.

All these stories are richly suggestive of family life and family passions. The story does not always revolve around erotic desire and jealousy between parent and child, however. Their diverse themes prompt
the question of whether a triangulated love affair between daughter
and mother and father is always the background story. It may be a
common story, at least in the construction of families within Western
cultures, but it is not necessarily a universal narrative. Some children
may not have such intense passions and their bond with parents may
be otherwise. Siblings, the neglected members of the family romance,
may be significant also as objects of love, even desire, and not simply
as objects of rivalry.

Downing argues that narratives of gods and goddesses give us (on
a grand scale) something "signally important: a simple acceptance that
human love takes many forms, among them the love of members of
one's own sex, and that this love has many faces" (1989:214). The need
to have one story to describe early development assumes a universal
course of development. This assumption is a fundamental problem.
Variations from a universal story can only be deviations—producing
deviants. Deviancy, the product of social construction, is always a matter of perception and a matter of politics. By limiting the developmental story to one, exemplifying it with a solitary myth chosen from
a wealth of narratives, the notion of a universal developmental route
is maintained. This story then becomes the yardstick by which all of
us are measured.

It is difficult to discuss dynamic development in women without
referring to oedipal and preoedipal periods. Theorists inevitably identify triangulated relations as oedipal and dyadic ones as preoedipal,
regardless of whether they recognize the inadequacy of the myth for
girls. I avoid this usage as much as possible and simply refer to triangular or dyadic relations, but when discussing other people's work, it
is often necessary to use their terminology.

There are advantages in using myths to understand human development when one recognizes them as emblematic of diversity rather than universality. These stories are about interactions between parents (or metaphorical parents) and children, not simply about children's fantasies and unconscious desires. They are interpersonal as well as intrapsychic signifiers. The stories recognize, as classical psychoanalysis generally does not, that parents continue to have fantasies, expectations, and unconscious desires in relation to their children and that their feelings and behavior significantly affect how the child goes through this time. These narratives also treat the child as participant in the drama, not merely as one who is acted upon.

Laius expects Oedipus to kill him and therefore sends him away to save himself. This abandonment creates the circumstances for their later encounter and makes it impossible for Oedipus to understand what he does. On the other hand, Oedipus is out on the road to avoid killing his father. He knows he carries the potential for patricide within himself. His passion, his competitiveness, his pride, and his desire go with him and propel him into the deed. Both parties, trying to control their fate, fail. This aspect of the story has traditionally (literarily speaking) been understood to hold this significance: it establishes independent action, action not influenced by another, as illusion.

2

Family Romances and Sexual Solutions

Analytic theory assumes that sexual preference arises out of the bond between mother and child, which then shifts—or does not shift—to the father. Social learning theorists see social and cultural values and experiences as significantly more influential. Much of the current developmental research suggests that many individual inclinations, including sexual ones, are inextricably linked to inborn responsive and perceptual preferences. Some of the first women analysts, such as Karen Horney (1926) and Melanie Klein (1928), also believed in a degree of biological determination for sexual choice. Unfortunately they assumed a universal biologically based heterosexuality, meaning that only distortions in female development (and contortions in psychoanalytic theory) could account for homosexuality. How much easier it would have been theoretically if they had similarly posited a biological basis when homosexuality prevailed. But they did not, and, for the most part, psychoanalytic theory has not entertained this possibility. At least one contemporary analyst, Richard Isay (1989), argues that male homosexuality is biologically determined; he suggests that the family dynamics associated with homosexuality follow from the family's response to the child's orientation rather than being the cause of it.

Psychoanalytic theory treats the family romance as universal, but perhaps it is not. All children's desires may not be so passionate or directed so intently toward the parents. For example, attachments to mothers and fathers are moderated by attachments to other siblings. Especially in large families, the parents' attention may be spread too thin to evoke a strong desire on the part of all the children. To what degree the child's desires are innate or are a matter of interpersonal dynamics, we do not know. Surely other variables operate as well. While the family romance is a common story, at least in Western European culture, it may not be a universal one.

Considering the many variables, internal and external, that influence human sexual potential, I find it necessary to assume that differences in choice of lovers—or, in psychoanalytic terms, object choice—ultimately depend upon multiple interactions. This chapter focuses on psychodynamic contributions to adult object choice but continues to reserve the place of other determinants. I also distinguish between sexual orientation or object choice and sexual identity.

Sexual Identity and Object Choice

Sexual identity is a term with many meanings, varying according to the user. Sometimes it refers to sexual orientation, sometimes to what others would call gender identity, and sometimes to a socially constructed identity, a label one gives oneself—*heterosexual, bisexual, lesbian,* or *gay.* In this last usage, a homosexual identity or a heterosexual identity is not necessarily equivalent to same-sex or opposite-sex object choice. Psychoanalytic and common usage tend to assume that identity and orientation will coincide, but for many individuals behavior, fantasies, and desires do not precisely match their identity or self-labeling.

As the Kinsey studies showed, many lesbians acknowledge some interest in men and many heterosexual women recognize in themselves some interest in other women (Kinsey et al. 1953). Some women are even virtually asexual but still identify as heterosexual or lesbian. There are women who state, "I'm not lesbian—I just happen to be in love with this woman," and women who identify as lesbian but have involvements with men. Do any of these possibilities really represent homosexuality or bisexuality—or are these even valid distinctions?

Identity is the synthesis of one's own self-perceptions with views of oneself perceived to be held by others (Cass 1984). Identity arises out of interactions between interpersonal experiences and intrapsychic ones: interpersonal experiences are interpreted in the light of intrapsychic structures and fantasies but they also alter internal structures in a dialectical relationship. The crises, conflicts, and resolutions of psychosexual development come from these experiences and these structures. Many lesbian-identified women might be considered bisexual in orientation. Others are what might be called primary lesbians, as *lesbian* describes both their identity and their desires (Ponse 1978; Golden 1987). Many heterosexually identified women also have some bisexual interests, but others could be called primary heterosexuals—they seem to have no homosexual interests.

One may understand object choice or sexual orientation as relatively fixed at an early age or as a more fluid construct capable of change over a lifetime. A person's sexual orientation can be conceptualized as "restricted and rigid" vs. "open and flexible" as well as in terms of preference for men or women (Richardson 1984). Those with a more rigid underlying orientation will be less susceptible to later influences and interactive experiences, while those whose sexuality is more fluid may experience shifts in sexual interests in the course of their lives. Sexual preferences may (or may not) be established at an early age, but sexual identity is generally not an issue until latency or adolescence, and it is obviously also open to change. Sexual orientation and sexual identity development may proceed on parallel tracks, each one influencing and organizing the other. Childhood, adolescent, and adult experiences are selected or deselected to help organize both desire and identity. Thus identity and orientation are interdependent, but separate, variables, and they may be incongruent.

Female Object Choice and the Failure of Psychoanalysis

Behind the complexity in the analytic literature about sexual development there still exists the default theory that human beings are naturally attracted to the opposite sex. Homosexuality has to be unnatural, then, and—the unstated corollary—heterosexuality cannot be. Few psychoanalysts bother to argue about this view—it is too obvious to doubt.[1] Clinical accounts in the psychoanalytic literature do not compare data between homosexuals and heterosexuals in treatment, nor are heterosexual outcomes viewed with suspicion.

Ideas about gender roles converge with those about sexuality: they line up squarely with conventional heterosexual arrangements. The understanding of gender and sexuality is tautological: a lesbian is masculine-identified because she is a lesbian, and she is a lesbian because she is masculine-identified. Observations of lesbians who do not fit this characterization (even in psychoanalytic case studies) are forgotten along with observations of masculinity in heterosexual women and the impossibility of defining masculinity in any way that endures social change.

Psychoanalytic theory does not explore variations in lesbianism. Female homosexuality means preoedipal fixation on the mother or foreclosure of interest in males; there is no way to understand women whose choice of lovers changes in midlife from men to women or from women to men. Some women come out of a long history of heterosexuality or a long-term marriage to decide they are interested in women for the first time. Some lesbians develop a new interest in male partners. There is clearly more fluidity to sexual choice than theory allows.

A model of sexual multiplicity is needed, one that considers differences between various homosexualities and heterosexualities, between primary and bisexual lesbians as well as between primary and bisexual heterosexual women. This chapter looks at a variety of family dynamics and their possible influence on (but not determination of) sexual choices. The next chapter considers possibilities of gender variation and multiplicity.

The Family Romance Revisited

Either lesbianism or heterosexuality may have different psychological meanings from one woman to another. Psychodynamically, lesbianism may be an expression of love and longing for the mother (or even another female member of the family—a sister, for example) or it may be founded on fear and rejection of the father. (Or a brother. In clinical practice I have worked with a woman who believed her lesbianism was partially determined by having had an extremely abusive older brother.) It may reflect discomfort with traditional gender roles or some alliance with feminist interests (the so-called elective lesbian).

Likewise heterosexuality may express love and longing for the father. (Or again, a brother. One heterosexual woman in therapy uncomfortably associated her relationships with men to a quasi-incestous bond with her brother). Or it may begin with fear and rejection of the mother. (Another heterosexual woman, also in therapy, described phobic [her word] reactions to intimacy with women, relating it to her intense and unresolved feelings from a suffocating relationship with her mother). It may reflect identification with traditional gender roles or a fear of not conforming to social norms. (Many women who come out later in life identify this fear as the source of their earlier heterosexuality. This raises the question of how many women remain in marriages, not questioning their heterosexuality, for this reason). A unitary theory of heterosexuality or homosexuality simply fails to match the diversity of sexual orientations one finds in clinical work, in empirical studies, or in everyday experience.

Relational theories understand psychodynamic development from an interpersonal and interactive perspective rather than a strictly intrapsychic one. What actually takes place between the parents and the child—not simply the wishes and fantasies of the child—matters. As Daniel Stern's research on early infant development reports, children "from the beginning mainly experience reality. . . . Reality experience precedes fantasy distortions in development" (1985:255). Tacit communication between parents and children is just as important as overt behavior. Parents and children both have many ways of communicating desires, preferences, approval, and disapproval.

The parents' bond with each other is another variable. Parents who are passionately attached to each other may leave little room for a child's desires. Parents who are hostile to each other may make desires feel dangerous, like choosing sides in a war. Parents who seem indifferent to each other make a child's own preference for one or the other burdened with more complex meaning than love or desire. The child may feel she must supply what is missing between them. When the parents' relationship is mutually respectful, the lucky child can internalize a relationship between equals and be comfortable there in her own relationships. When the parents' relationship is one-sided, abusive, or disengaged, the child is vulnerable to identifying with one at the expense of the other and to repeating some version of their relationship in her own.

Helene Deutsch's (1944) account of female development identified a strong bisexual component in many women's sexuality. She wrote that the little girl's turn to the father was not exclusive, it simply came to be more intense than her attachment to her mother. Nancy Chodorow (1978) developed this idea more fully and argued that the usual romantic triangle, even for most heterosexual women, is a bisexually divided one rather than a heterosexually tilted one. Female sexuality is perhaps also not as genitally focused as male sexuality; it may be an elaboration of relational interests and inseparable from them. This view of female development is akin to the Persephone story. From this perspective, later developmental factors can play a more significant role and the larger world of extended family, friends, other significant adults, and social institutions can contribute to sexual identity.

Psychodynamic theory considers only the influence of the romance between parents and children, not other relationships or influences. Even restricting oneself to this arena, one sees broad differences in experience that might shape different outcomes. A daughter expresses her interests as they emerge, and her parents respond, separately and together, in some way. If the daughter is inherently drawn more strongly to one parent or another (as a consequence of either psychological or biological influences), her preference is somehow expressed in the family interactions and undoubtedly shapes parents' responses in turn. Chodorow (1978) reminded us that a daughter's interest in the father is only one side of the equation; the father's response is equally important. Likewise different mothers are capable of different levels of responsiveness to a daughter's wooing. The parents' reactions require the daughter to meet them somewhere, on some mutually created ground. Thus she learns strategic and defensive ways of handling their responses to her.

Here I suggest some of the possibilities simply to demonstrate the multiplicity of experience that lies behind the false dichotomy between heterosexuality and homosexuality. Female sexuality may be seen as a continuum, such as the one Kinsey theorized, from exclusive heterosexuality to exclusive homosexuality. Any point on the continuum might involve a measure of defensive strategy, but no position is necessarily or inevitably pathological. I use examples of common scenarios in the family drama to speculate about dynamic pathways that are later expressed as heterosexuality but reflect diverse underlying concerns. I also speculate about various paths of lesbian development. How do some daughters keep the mother as primary love interest without being bound to her? Either way, how can the mother become an Other, someone separate and distinct from the daughter, without a turn away from her? In all cases, these are descriptive outlines of dynamic processes rather than explanation of causes. They address the question of how sexuality might be shaped in a particular way within the family rather than attempt to answer definitive and impossible questions of etiology.

In the ideal family story the mother enjoys her daughter's romance with her—they are mutually entranced. The mother also supports and encourages various turns of the child's development. When the daughter becomes interested in the father (assuming heterosexual parents here), the mother doesn't feel her own attachment threatened. The father, in turn, may match the mother's appeal through his solid presence and his person. He enjoys his daughter's interest in him without threat; he is not inclined toward either rejection or seduction and he does not desire her to abandon the mother. In this scenario the daughter may retain bisexual interests—although later experiences might tilt her behavior and identity in one direction or another.

In actuality, of course, it is hard to conceive of a path of psychosexual development that does not include any defensive strategies.

Such moves may be adaptive and progressive, however, rather than pathological and regressive. Furthermore, the father isn't always able to compete with the mother's appeal, and an altogether different route of development may occur. From the various possibilities, a multiplicity of sexualities emerges, differently based heterosexualities and homosexualities.

First of all, mothers can have conflicts of their own over sexuality. They are sometimes inhibited in their response to a daughter's wooing. The mother's homophobia, or fear of her own homoerotic feelings (or simply of erotic feelings of any kind), may make her especially uneasy with a daughter's erotic interest (Flax 1978; Caplan 1981). The daughter may feel rejected and turn to her father as a kind of consolation prize. Heterosexuality becomes an appealing defensive move. Of course some daughters redouble their pursuit in the face of rejection. Longing for the mother may become the dominant feature in the daughter's psychosexual development. This desire may be played out in adult years as a pathological attraction to relationships full of ambivalence or rejection, or it may find some resolution in mutually appreciated love, perhaps with another woman. In either outcome—heterosexual or homosexual—the problem is not with the sex of her object choice but with the damage to the daughter's sense of self.

When the mother's homophobia is part of the unspoken relationship between mother and daughter, it engenders a sense of an erotically rejected self. This rejection may be incorporated through projective identification into the daughter's unconscious structuring of her sexual feelings. Thus the transmission of cultural fears and values takes place unconsciously as well as through conscious communication about them. This communication can prevail regardless of the final outcome of the daughter's sexual development, and in clinical work with a female therapist both lesbian and heterosexual patients sometimes find this rejected self emerging in the transference (chapter 4 discusses this dilemma for the daughter more fully).

The daughter may also turn to the father to get some emotional distance from the mother. If the mother-daughter relationship is too enmeshed, this move may be a necessary defense, a kind of psychic wedge against the mother. Chodorow describes the girl's rejection of her mother as "a defense against primary identification . . . attempting by fiat to establish boundaries between herself and her mother" (1978:124). The daughter's defenses may quench any continuing interest in the mother (identity and desire not being so clearly distinct as theory would have it). This kind of heterosexuality may be fiercely held and any homosexual interests rejected because they threaten this boundary.

On the other hand, if the daughter is able to differentiate herself from her mother without this defensive turn, she may have a more resilient sense of self. That is, if the daughter comes to experience her differentness from the mother through the mother's tolerance of differentiation and with help from the father or connections with other significant people, she may be able to grasp the mother as other in a nontraumatic way and her erotic interest in her may continue. I'll return to this possibility later.

If the mother is unable to help her daughter enter the world of sexuality, the daughter may find her inadequate for this reason rather than for her anatomy. It is not the mother's lack of a penis but her lack of a sexual self that sends the daughter looking elsewhere. She may idealize the father as someone who can function with greater ease sexually and, through his attention to her, come to value her own sexual powers. The problem for this daughter is whether her sexuality is her own, whether it is subjectively held, or whether she knows her sexuality primarily through being the object of someone else's (the father's, the man's) desire.

When one thinks of the father's role, there are other questions. It is possible that the father will be more attractive to the daughter than the mother—by virtue of a greater capacity for nurturing, a greater interest in or identification with the daughter, more appealing physical or psychological qualities, or his greater power in the family politics. He may eclipse the mother's role, and the daughter's homosexual interests may not develop very far. Her relationship with her mother may be conflictual or carry a sense of missing connections. Like the myth of Athena, the daughter of the swallowed-up mother, she may be father-identified or androgynous. Again, her sexual interests may lack subjectivity or a life of their own. Sexuality may become subordinate to other concerns, and she may experience herself as relatively asexual. Or identity with the father may include identity with his sexual desire, and she develops an active sexuality, one that sometimes throws her into conflict with her gendered sense of self.

Another concern within the father-daughter relationship is the degree to which the father needs to shape the daughter's development in a typically feminine way. Some research suggests that fathers, more than mothers, are concerned with gender conformity in their children. They are more likely to expect and reward traditional femininity in their daughters and to discourage or disapprove of nontraditional behaviors, especially as the daughter's romantic interest appears (Johnson 1975). The daughter's response may be acquiescence, sealing the erotic/romantic bond between them on the father's terms. She accepts the conventional view of femininity, with its limitations to her potential. If she reacts against this expectation, however, she may be left wounded and wary. She may identify with the father, seeking an alternative bond with him, and be like the mythic goddesses who see heterosexuality as a form of bondage. Perhaps she will find lesbianism, with its greater acceptance of gender nonconformity, more appealing.

On the other hand, what if the father fails to take much interest in his daughter? Worse, what if he is seductive and threatens her physical and psychological well-being? The father's inadequacy leaves the daughter with difficult options. If things are well with the mother, she may pursue this connection with the mother exclusively—but nevertheless retain a sense of rejection. Or, like the mother-rejected daughter, she might redouble her efforts and dedicate herself to the pursuit of the father (of a man) to repair this wound. Longing for the father shapes her erotic interests and may also be played out in adult years in attractions to unavailable lovers—of whatever sex.

However, what if the father does not attract the daughter as much as the mother does? Perhaps he is unnurturing or too unavailable, too rough, etc., to sustain the daughter's deepest interests. Or perhaps the daughter is simply (innately) more oriented toward the mother. In

this case the daughter may persevere in her erotic-emotional attachment to her mother. What happens with the daughter whose attraction to her mother continues to overshadow an interest in the father?
Can she still effect the necessary separation from her mother? Boys
manage to do this, but they disidentify themselves from the mother to
do it. Something must shift in the mother-daughter relationship also
for the girl's development to continue. Thomas Ogden (1989) has for-
mulated a theory of heterosexual female development that is more
benign than Freud's proposition. In his ideas I find something else as
well: how the girl's development may continue without a switch from
mother to father.

A Transitional Romance

Like others, Ogden criticizes traditional theory because it provides no
basis for healthy love relationships for women, relationships based on
something other than disappointment in the mother. In his view the
daughter separates from the mother by using her as a transitional
object, not by turning away from her. The transition at issue here is
from undifferentiated love to love based on differentiation between
self and other, two who are more or less separate and whole rather
than fused and incomplete. The transition allows the mother to
emerge as Other (rather than as extension of self), an eroticized Other
with her own center of experience rather than a caretaker. Ogden
employs Winnicott's idea of the transitional object as something that
is "both reality and fantasy; both me and not-me" (1989:117); the
mother is still omnipotent, protective, and internal but also becomes
external, someone with her own internal life. This is a momentous
event in development, a grand achievement on the child's part, but
one that is never absolute and complete. A successful transition here
allows the child's psychic world to expand—to include externality
and separateness without giving up what preceded it.

According to Odgen, the mother responds to her daughter's romance with her by drawing upon her own unconscious childhood
romance in which she began to fall in love with her father. Through

this relationship she knows what the daughter needs and plays out the role of father for the daughter. This allows the daughter to experiment with her growing interest in the father via the safety of her established romance with her mother.

Ogden writes:

> This reorganization takes place non-traumatically because it is mediated by a relationship with the mother that embodies the following paradox: *the little girl falls in love with the mother-as-father and with the father-as-mother.* . . . The role of mother as oedipal transitional object is to allow herself to be loved as a man (her own unconscious identification with her own father). In so doing, she unconsciously says to her daughter, "If I were a man, I would be in love with you, find you beautiful and would very much want to marry you." (119–120)

The transitional experience allows the daughter to participate in an erotic-romantic relationship with an other, without in fact giving up the mother as subjective object. Eventually an actual other—in Ogden's version, the father, of course will take this place for the daughter as someone who "lives beyond the realm of the little girl's omnipotence." In this transitional relationship the mother sanctions the little girl's love of her father and eventually, other men. The transitional relationship depends upon the mother's comfort in engaging in an identification as male, being able to experience the "dialectical inter-play between masculine and feminine identities" in a creative way.

Nothing in Ogden's account is dependent on gender however. In fact the distinction between genders is necessarily blurred. Because he frames his theory in heterosexual terms, Ogden describes the mother's role as stand-in for the father. What is essential is that the mother allows herself to participate in play with her daughter, being able to be an other by drawing upon her own internalized parent-child romance. The daughter initiates this shift through her gradual readiness to perceive the mother as other. The mother responds in kind with her capacity to enjoy being an other for her daughter, someone other than the caretaking mother.

The mother may mediate her daughter's transition to a relationship with an other based on her own internalized romance with mother or father. In other words, through their relationship, the mother unconsciously communicates to the child a message that (paralleling Ogden's account) might go something like this, "I can enjoy this romance with you as if I were someone who could choose you too." She plays the role of an other, separate and external, just as well this way. She shifts from being a subjective object, in Winnicott's terms, to an objectively perceived external and whole person.

This "as-if" play grants the daughter permission to fall in love with other real, external figures. In this transitional relationship the mother and child may play with both of the possibilities. The distinctions between heterosexual and homosexual love may not be so sharp or important here. Only later are they sorted out more clearly as the child does move on to actual others. The mother's awareness of herself in two simultaneous relationships with her daughter, knowing that she is separate, is other, from her daughter, but also experiencing the oneness between them, makes the child's simultaneous dual experience possible. She is appropriately reflected in both positions.

The child is then free to experience eroticized attachments to other females: relatives, teachers, family friends. The triangulation of mother, child, and other may occur in many stages with various stand-ins. Little girls have crushes on older women with great frequency, often greater than on male teachers, neighbors, or relatives. The mother's participation in this romance may be largely unconscious or at least unacknowledged. It may even take place side by side with her discomfort about homosexual love.

Major object-relations theorists (Klein, Winnicott, Mahler) do not base the capacity for mature object-relatedness upon heterosexuality. Instead, they invoke the child's growing awareness of external reality and the mother's separateness. Transitional objects help to mediate this shift by attenuating the anxiety it arouses: too much anxiety could disrupt a necessarily gradual integration of awareness of external reality.

Ogden, too, argues not that whole object relations are dependent upon heterosexual development but simply that a shift is required from mother as subjective object to external object. In his account of male oedipal development, Ogden emphasizes that the boy is shifting from one mother to another: "the Oedipal mother is and is not the same mother the little boy loved, hated and feared prior to his discovery of her (and his father) as external Oedipal objects" (1989:142). The girl may make a parallel shift that leaves her romantic love for the mother still the dominant force in her psychosexual development.

This perspective permits an understanding of primary lesbianism as an alternative route of sexual development, one more continuous with earlier experience. The father's presence, for whatever reason, may fail to supplant the love relationship to the mother. It may remain as a relatively unelaborated intrapsychic configuration or it may gain further interest at a later point in development. Neither outcome indicates arrested development, however, any more than the heterosexual boy's transition from preoedipal to oedipal love of the mother does.

Separation-Individuation and Sexual Identity

The emergence of sexual identity often begins in adolescence, although some people remember grappling with the issue much earlier, and for many it does not become an issue until much later (Cass 1979; Burch 1992). When identity does become an issue, it interacts with the processes of separation and individuation. In an internal sense, claiming homosexuality as an identity usually means differentiating or disidentifying from both parents. Externally—that is, actually revealing this information to parents—coming out entails high risk: anything from disapproval to alienation and utter rejection. An individual beginning to take on such an identity inevitably takes another step on the path of separation.

Few lesbians or gay men have homosexual parents. Because sexual identity is a highly privileged cultural and psychological signifier, this disjunction from parents occurs at a deep level of self experience. Coming out to oneself, as it is sometimes referred to, can be felt as cutting loose from all familiar moorings, generating a profound sense of individual vulnerability. This disjunction is likely to occur at a social level as well, but there at least one has the possibility of finding allies. Next to one's self-awareness of sexual identity, coming out to parents is almost always the most significant act within the process of coming out.

Indeed parents often experience it themselves as an act of defiance, as something intentionally perpetrated against them rather than something primarily about who their child is. Parents often strongly resist this kind of differentiation and insist they are unable to understand or relate to it in any way (cf. Weston 1991). Not uncommonly, they treat differentiation of this kind not as separation, but as severance. The child (who may be an adult now) is someone with whom *they* can no longer identify, and this may be intolerable to *them*. When children (adolescent or adult) come out to parents, it is a profound challenge to the parents' own success in separation-individuation.

But of course it is primarily a crisis for the lesbian or gay person who is coming out. The child may experience coming out as individuation—asserting her "true self"—but she finds that her parents treat it as rejection and/or reject her in kind. In early development rejection or punishment is the most disastrous response to the child's efforts to individuate; it is perhaps only slightly less devastating for the adolescent. Many lesbians and gay men do manage to weather this crisis. Many postpone it for years. Some never attempt it.

The fact that so many do manage it under such adverse conditions, however, speaks to the question of whether homosexuality indicates an early developmental failure. Only with some measure of success in handling differentiation processes can an individual take on such a challenge. If homosexuals are inevitably perpetuating symbiotic ties to parents of the same sex, it is hard to conceive of how they may at the same time tolerate such a profound degree of disidentification and alienation from the parent who has never become other to them. On the contrary, they would be more likely never to develop any sexual identity.

Weathering the vicissitudes of coming out not only requires a successful foundation, it may also help to consolidate psychological separation from the parents and individuation. For some it feels like the ultimate act of growing up (cf. Stanley and Wolfe 1980; Weston 1991), knowing that one can live fully independent of one's parents if necessary. When a family reconciliation is possible afterward, the experience is especially confirming of self. Acceptance by the family on one's own terms usually clarifies that separation does not mean severance, it is not absolute independence but a reordering of familial relationships. Coming out can further development at an individual level regardless of outcome, but a positive resolution within family ties is particularly fortuitous.

Adult sexual interests do not line up in a neat correlation with one's relationship with the parent of a given gender. The heterosexual woman's relationship with her father is not the only influence on her relationships with men. Her relationship with her mother, for better or worse, may also be transferred over to male partners. The same is true of lesbian and bisexual women. Adult relationships are not a simple replication of childhood ones.

The relationship with a given parent does not seem to decide definitively whom the child will love as an adult. In some cases perhaps biology overrides all else, and a heterosexually inclined child will commingle all her experiences with her parents in those with adult partners. Likewise for lesbians. Sometimes gender may seem altogether irrelevant. For example, in the course of therapy one woman left a twenty-year marriage to a man and became involved with another woman. The marriage seemed to express her relationship with her mother, while the lesbian relationship felt more like her relationship with her father. In psychodynamic terms, she had found a father who behaved like her mother, then switched to a mother who behaved like her father.

The influence of the various family dramas I described is necessarily a fiction, an organizing device for imagining how adult love experiences might be shaped by childhood ones in the family. Relationships with mothers inevitably color later relationships, influencing but not determining the sex of one's lovers. Experiences with fathers often translate into potent expectations, or transferences, with later male partners—but not always. They also affect relationships with female partners.

Like myths and like fiction, these descriptions attempt to capture some truth without being true in a factual sense. If human sexuality is to some degree biologically predetermined, to some degree culturally constructed, and (as a subcategory of the second) given shape within the family, then one can use psychodynamic theory to see how the family alters and elaborates on what may already be emerging. It assumes that humans are almost endlessly inventive and resourceful in how they manage the circumstances presented to them.

Different formulations suggest different qualitative routes to adult choices. The route to heterosexual love may be defensive, or favorable conditions may open up a relatively unconflicted avenue for this shift. The same possibilities exist for routes toward homosexuality. Desiring men, desiring women, or both—any of these possibilities may emerge along with a capacity for whole relationships. Any of these may involve defensive maneuvers interacting with innately emerging developmental shifts.

When there is an underlying bisexual orientation, as I think is true for many women, the sex of the partner(s) actually chosen may be particularly amenable to social and situational influences, since internal options are more fluid. Some of these women come to identify as heterosexual, some as lesbian, and some are bisexually identified. The theories proposed by social and behavioral psychologists illuminate how situational influences interact with a person's psychosexual potential at a given stage in development. The point is that no one view is complete, and there are divergent routes on the way toward final object choice. The road toward heterosexuality is not a straight one, and we cannot regard other destinations as a wrong turn.

The concepts of oedipal failure or success are problematic. One's positive sense of self and capacity for full relatedness are the salient issues, not the gender of one's attachments, and there are degrees of failure and success within any sexual orientation. Robert Stoller expresses the problem one way:

What evidence is there that heterosexuality is less complicated than homosexuality, less the product of infantile-childhood struggles to master trauma, conflict, frustration, and the like? As a result of innumerable analyses, the burden of proof . . . has shifted to those who use the heterosexual as the standard of health, normality, mature genital characterhood, or whatever other ambiguous criterion serves one's philosophy these days. . . . Thus far, the counting, if it is done from published reports, puts the heterosexual and the homosexual in a tie: 100 percent abnormals. (1985:101–102)

Finally, this analysis raises questions about the definition of pathology itself. Exactly what a healthy person is, or what defines healthy sexuality, is difficult to state. Typically the answer is framed in terms of two dimensions: the degree of deviation from social norms and the degree of psychological suffering in an individual life. These dimensions are themselves always confounded by cultural values that vary enormously in different societies and at different times within the same society. Whole societies may be seen as themselves pathological, based on political or religious forces repellent to those outside (or inside) them.

What then characterizes a healthy person? This question constitutes a philosophical dilemma that most theorists can only recognize. It serves to caution us against an authoritative attitude in descriptions of health and pathology. In this vein Stoller writes:

Beware the concept "normal." It is beyond the reach of objectivity. It tries to connote statistical validity but hides brute judgments on social and private goodness that, if admitted, would promote honesty and modesty we do not yet have in patriots, lawmakers, psychoanalysts, and philosophers. (41)

Relinquishing the focus on who is normal and who is not and instead trying to understand what works best for a given individual, one may conclude that homosexuality and heterosexuality both require more exploration. Traditional psychoanalytic thinking linked with historical and cultural prejudices about masculinity, femininity, and homosexuality exert a pull of their own, somewhat like a gravitational field. It is unthinkable, really, that anyone's sexual development is entirely free of trauma, adverse influences, necessary compromises, and strategic resolutions. We require a wider view of human sexual development, one that considers these strategic resolutions to be a triumph of the psyche's creative potential rather than pathology.

3

Gender Identities, Lesbianism, and Potential Space

The relationship between gender identity and sexual orientation is another area of psychoanalytic thinking still entangled with sociocultural paradigms that prevailed decades ago. Gender and sexuality are particularly difficult topics to explore freely, bound up as they are with our deepest psychological and social needs. Psychoanalytic theory should require us to assume that our relatively fixed ideas about gender and sexuality do not reflect a natural order.

Contemporary psychoanalytic writers address gender identity and object choice as separate but related constructs, but they continue to treat them as congruent with stereotypical gender arrangements. For example, when Phyllis Tyson (1982) traces distinct developmental lines for core gender identity, gender role, and object choice, she joins them together under the concept of "global" gender identity. In her view, by virtue of object choice, a male homosexuality inevitably reflects something feminine in the psyche and lesbianism inevitably expresses masculinity.

Psychoanalytic writings have associated lesbian development in particular with masculinity (McDougall 1980, 1989; Socarides 1968, 1981). And the meaning of "masculine identification" in psychoanalytic theory has shifted: once it designated specific qualities and attributes, now it signifies a disturbance in gender identity and is synonymous with female homosexuality (cf. Magee and Miller 1992). From this perspective lesbianism does not signify a female-to-female connection at all, but instead a male-identified woman who seeks a woman for herself. True homosexuality does not really exist, only distorted heterosexuality.

Initially Freud (1905) accepted Havelock Ellis's account of homosexuality as gender inversion, but in "The Psychogenesis of a Case of Homosexuality in a Woman" (Freud 1920) he repudiated it. There he argued that "mental sexual character and object choice do not necessarily coincide" (170). Still later, however, in his "Female Sexuality" (1931), he again concluded that a masculinity complex underlay a lesbian object choice.

Empirical evidence from social psychology tells the gender story somewhat differently. This research suggests that when lesbians' gender roles and identities are compared with heterosexual women's, lesbians lean more toward "androgyny" than masculinity (Jones and DeCecco 1982; LaTorre and Wendenburg 1983). For example, one study showed a more highly developed sense of "masculinity" in lesbians than in heterosexual women, but an equally developed sense of "femininity" in the two groups (Oldham, Farnil, and Ball 1982). Androgyny is a misleading term, however, if it implies a smooth integration of masculine and feminine identifications. I suggest that what is being documented here is instead the configuration of alternate identifications within an individual.

When the feminist movement challenged traditional gender roles in heterosexual relationships, it simultaneously challenged the idea of role-playing in lesbian couples. Many studies have supported this challenge by demonstrating how rarely stereotyped roles occur in lesbian relationships (Bell and Weinberg 1978; Blumstein and Schwartz 1983; Jay and Young 1977; Schneider 1986). Other studies found that lesbians prefer relationships where there is an absence of role-playing and that equality between partners is the norm for most lesbian couples.[1] (The more complex question of what equality consists of and how it is also problematic for lesbians is the subject of chapter 6.) These studies suggest that analytic theorists will misunderstand lesbian relationships if the only context available is the normative picture of heterosexuality. The limitations of current theory regarding gender identifications and object choice are particularly evident in psycho-analytic accounts of clinical work with lesbians. Lesbian relationships exist within their own somewhat distinct culture; they find their own meanings and can best be understood there. This cultural reference point is generally lacking in psychoanalysis—not only for lesbians but for others as well.

Gender identities of women who are lesbian (viewed reluctantly as a group) may differ in certain ways from gender identities of hetero-sexual women (an equally misleading grouping). For lesbians the gen-dered sense of self may be more fluid than for heterosexual women, shifting between various representations and expressions of masculine and feminine identities. Lesbian partners employ this fluidity in vari-ous complementary ways that show a creative use of self and other. Their interpersonal dynamics may expand each woman's sense of gendered self rather than (or in addition to) confirming it. Lesbian relationships offer certain advantages precisely because they hold the potential for this kind of exchange. To understand such fluidity as advantageous rather than as signifying developmental problems, we need to consider postmodernist thinking about gender. Postmodern-ism challenges the unitary conception of the self upon which psycho-analysis and psychology in general have relied. It particularly under-mines notions of gender as essential, fixed, and universal.

Identities: Origins and Functions

Gender identity is defined as "a gendered sense of self" or "an inter-nal self-evaluation of maleness or femaleness," distinct from Stoller's idea of core gender identity, which is a "recognition of belonging to a biological category" (Schwartz 1986:58). Psychoanalytic and other psychological theories argue that one's gender identity is based on early identifications with a given parent, who may or may not be the same sex as oneself (Fast 1990). Social constructionists understand gender as developing in social interactions throughout one's life based on prevailing cultural categories (Ortner and Whitehead 1984). Gender identification as discussed here is largely a conscious sense of self in cultural terms or what some have called "gender role identity" (Schwartz 1986).

Many lesbians describe themselves as having been tomboys when they were kids or as not properly feminine in some way. How many heterosexual women have also felt unfeminine? Awareness of gender improprieties often precedes awareness of sexual interests. Possibly this experience shapes or reinforces sexual choices in some way, without exactly determining it, but surely the reverse is also true: awareness of lesbian interests affects one's gendered self-image—although not in a readily predictable way.

Postmodern feminist and Lacanian psychoanalytic thinkers argue that the category of gender itself is a social construction, the terms of which are decreed by patriarchal law. Jane Flax (1990) points out that

> through gender relations two types of persons are created: males and females, each posited as an exclusionary category. . . . The actual content of being male or female and the rigidity of the categories themselves are highly variable across cultures and time . . . [and] have been (more or less) relationships of domination. (22)

Judith Butler (1990b) notes that feminist psychoanalytic theorists attempt to integrate the male and female spheres, representing autonomy and nurturance respectively, while other feminist psychodynamic writers (presumably those like the Stone Center theorists [Jordan et al. 1991]) establish the feminine as an alternative, as a subject who defines herself relationally and is different from the masculine because she does not fear dependency. Either approach conceives of "a normative model of a unified self," androgynous in the one case, specifically feminine ("organized by a founding maternal identification"; Butler 1990b:328) in the other, but a coherent unified gendered self either way.

In contrast, Butler undertakes a radical deconstruction of gender. She negates the idea of a unified or coherent gender identity, replacing it with a fluidity of identities:

Within the terms of psychoanalytic theory, then, it is quite possible to understand gendered subjectivity as a history of identifications, parts of which can be brought into play in given contexts and which, precisely because they encode the contingencies of personal history, do not always point back to an internal coherence of any kind. (331)

This understanding, she points out, is expressed through gender parodies such as drag performance (or, I would add, butch/femme identities): "In imitating gender, drag implicitly reveals the imitative structure of gender itself. . . . The notion of gender parody here does not assume that there is an original which such parodic identities imitate. Indeed, the parody is of the very notion of an original" (338).

Thoroughly bound within the confines of social law, we cannot abandon the notion of gender identity. We use such ideas and identities (which are, as Butler reminded us, simply fantasies themselves) to organize and make meaning of our experience, within the limits of our cultural allowances. Encounters with other cultures are unsettling. They remind us how much of what we take for granted—such as the notion of gender and anatomy as mutually identified—is not constant cross culturally.[2]

Recent psychoanalytic thinking has incorporated notions of fluidity and multiplicity with gendered experience. Adrienne Harris asserts that gender may be "core and coherent" but can also "mutate, dissolve, and prove irrelevant or insubstantial" (1991:197). For my purposes, however, her work is limited by its implication that alternate gender identifications determine object choice, which is only one of the possible associations between them. Virginia Goldner questions whether "the presumption that an internally consistent gender identity is possible or even desirable" (1991:250). Further, she states that

consolidating a stable gender identity is a developmental accomplishment that requires the activation of pathological processes, insofar as any gender-incongruent thought, act, impulse, mood, or trait would have to be disowned, displaced, (mis)placed (as in projective identification), split off . . . Since gender is a psychic

and cultural configuration of the self that "cleanses" itself of
opposing tendencies, it is, by definition, a universal, false-self system generated in compliance with the rule of the two-gender
system. (258–259)

Her thinking points toward the rich developmental possibilities inherent in relationships that invite a loosening of "compliance with the
rule," a point central to this chapter.

Cultural allowances function on behalf of political dynamics or, as
Flax said of gender, relationships of domination. Limits that provide
organization and meaning to our experience are not comfortably
changed; power relations do not shift without great resistance. Nevertheless, there is always someone at the edge, pressing the limit further
until new social law is generated. Regarding gender, the more radical
homosexual presses this limit. As some have argued, cultural fears of
gender variation may be the bedrock of homophobia (Person 1988;
Wilson 1984). We all, radical and conformist alike, live to some extent
within the same social rules, and those who defy, negate, or ignore
them suffer their individual penalties. Those who try but inevitably
fail to meet social requirements about gender (as everyone does to
some degree) devise their own solutions and resolutions.

Gender Identities: Transitions and Ambiguities

There is in everyone some degree of identification with both parents,
which allows the child to embody both genders within the self, what
Joyce McDougall (1986) discusses as our psychic bisexuality, our wish
to *be* as well as to possess the opposite-sex parent. Irene Fast (1990)
suggests that before children undergo gender differentiation, maleness
and femaleness are not experienced as mutually exclusive categories.
As anatomical differences are observed and gender categories are differentiated, masculinity and femininity become opposites, not merely
in anatomy but also in behaviors and personal characteristics associated with them. Assignment of gender brings a profound sense of limitation. This account again omits the crucial awareness that culture has

already determined gender's meaning, and the child is acculturated by sorting out gender "appropriateness." We may ask why it is necessary that anatomical differences carry such psychological limitations.

In the endeavor to articulate a more adequate conception of gender identities in lesbian women, I draw upon both clinical experience and interviews with lesbians. The interviews, which addressed lesbian relationships (Burch 1992), afforded me an opportunity to explore the question of gender. Eight individual women and four couples, all between the ages of thirty-six and fifty-two, were interviewed for approximately one to one and a half hours. The value of these informal interviews is purely descriptive. They are not necessarily representative of other lesbians, of course, but these women's self-reflective comments yield another account of how gender develops and is expressed. The interviews focused on conscious narratives of gender, but they allowed me to explore the subject more freely than in clinical work. Two specific questions related to gender: (a) "How do you experience your family ties and alignments—that is, in your family whom do you identify with or feel close to?" and (b) "How do you think about or identify with the terms *butch* and *femme*?"

When I asked where they felt their family alignments were, these women's responses covered all the possibilities, a wide range of identifications and disidentifications with mothers, fathers, brothers, and sisters; there was no shape or pattern evident. A number of women spoke of shifting identifications, from mother to father (or vice versa), as they moved into adolescence, reflecting that "history of identifications" to which Butler referred. Marty, a thirty-nine-year-old Latina woman raised in rural California, described the correspondence of these shifts with family resemblances:

I grew up as a tomboy. I think I was identified with my dad for a couple of reasons. My older sister looks like my mom a lot. I'm built very much like my dad, and I have his darker coloring. So I was sort of my father's daughter. Also my parents clearly wanted a son by the time I came along. By default I became the tomboy for Dad. It feels like it suited me. I loved being outdoors, and my sister didn't. But there were also lots of ways I got reinforced for it. So I was the one who went fishing with my dad, and I really looked up to him. I'm still very close to my father. He's very nurturing. I admire and enjoy him. But as I got older. . . . I'd always been close to my mother in another way. My mother is a very powerful personality, in good and bad ways, so our relationship was more ambivalent. She was very attached to me and protective of me. By the time I got to junior high, my face started looking more like my mother's, and I clearly enjoyed, as I became more feminine, a closer relationship with her. I identified more with her then than with my father.

This account suggests the diversity of factors, both conscious and unconscious, that determine identifications: genetics, social conditioning, emotional bonding, and family needs and projections. It also describes a fluid identity, which may be encountered in pieces, corresponding to the postmodernist conception and unlike the unified and "continuous rather than discrete" (Schwartz, 1986:58) identity psychological theories favor.

In response to this question about identities and alignments within their families, many women described how one or both parents did not embody conventional gender roles. Some women explicitly described a parent as androgynous. Others identified the father as the nurturing one in the family, sometimes as the passive one, or the mother as more instrumental or more authoritative. Often this was experienced as a positive thing, a particular asset found in their family that other families lacked. Sometimes it was an unhappy situation, for example, when the mother was domineering and the father ineffectual.

As I considered this finding, it seemed to me that these women intuitively felt they had been granted some flexibility about gender through their parents' more androgynous personalities. At the same time, some of them mentioned that their siblings were extremely traditional in their gender roles. What enables one child to find opportunity for herself in a family trait, while another reacts against it, defies generalization. Nevertheless, it seemed clear that for the women I interviewed their parents' variations were important to their own sense of gendered self.

Both lesbian and heterosexual women may experience themselves as masculine in important ways that have nothing to do with confusion about gender identity and may be either highly valued or felt as deviant. When Paula, a white thirty-four-year-old woman raised in an upper-middle-class East Coast family, described the complex interaction of familial and social influences on her experience of gender, Butler's reference to the "contingencies of personal history" was apparent:

When I was first a lesbian I would have identified fiercely as a "butch." That was less about sexuality and more about presenting a tough, armored image to the world. The message I got in my family was that a woman is not the thing to be. Period. I looked at my brother and my sister and saw how my parents treated them. If I had a choice here, clearly I would not choose to be a woman. So I think I had a tremendous identification with my brother and adopted a lot of his mannerisms. None of this was conscious at the time. . . . Being "butch," being a construction worker . . . was a way to say "I'm identifying with the power here." Part of my process has been to soften a lot. What I wear has completely changed in the twelve years that I've been a lesbian. If I look feminine now, it's okay.

When a woman claims masculinity as her own prerogative, this may reflect identification with males, as this woman's story relates. It is nevertheless a different story from that of a man with this same identification because the woman simultaneously retains a core identity as female. Again, as this woman makes clear, masculinity embodied in a woman may generate a new, and in some ways reparative, experience of the feminine.

A fundamental signifier of femininity in our culture, the desire to bear a child, is also common to lesbians. Formerly, lesbians had chil-

dren in heterosexual marriages before they came out. Now many lesbians choose to have children with a lesbian partner, through donor
insemination, adoption, or other means. Five of the eight women I
interviewed individually had children (three within a heterosexual
marriage, two with a lesbian partner), another is considering pregnancy, and another is co-parent of her partner's children. Only one
woman felt she did not want to have children, and even she was
unsure. Two of the four couples had children. Mary Anne Kirk-
patrick's research on lesbian families and Joyce McDougall's clinical
studies of lesbians in treatment also found the desire to bear children
as strong as in heterosexual women (Wolfson 1984). This desire in
itself challenges either the equation between masculinity and lesbianism or the equation between gender and desire to bear children.

For some lesbians the experiences of pregnancy and child rearing
expand gender possibilities. A brief clinical example illustrates this. A
woman in her late thirties, who identified as a lesbian, struggled in
therapy with understanding in what ways she embodied and valued
masculinity and femininity in herself. She preferred to wear jeans and
short hair, but she kept her hair longer because she didn't like to look
too masculine. When she became pregnant conflicts and doubts about
her femininity were more accessible and her work progressed. During
this time she indulged herself, as she put it, in a very short haircut,
which she loved. For her this meant the conflict had found resolution;
both femininity and masculinity were hers, as she chose them. For this
brief period she could visibly reveal a more complex expression of her
gender experience, the "contradictions" coexisting.

Gender Roles in Lesbian Relationships

In the terms of much of psychoanalytic and popular literature, there
is the *butch*, the pseudomasculine lesbian who takes the part of the
male lover in both behavior and dress, and the *femme,* who is not quite
a true woman, being lesbian, but a caricature of femininity: helpless,
narcissistic, hysterical, maternal, or wifely. Through their mimicry of
heterosexual love they may find some measure of satisfaction. The

concepts of butch and femme linger, often a matter of parody or in-group humor that nevertheless carries real meaning. The fact that lesbians both deny these roles and continue to be interested in them led me to inquire about them in the interviews.

When I asked women whether they used or identified with these terms, all but one said no. However, many understood two levels of meaning here. The caricatured conception of butch and femme just described did not interest them, but the need for a way to express their different sense of gendered self—different from conventional feminine or masculine roles—did interest them. For example, several women used terms like *butchy femme* or *femmy butch* to describe themselves or their partner. One woman said, "I always felt more identified as femme, although I think I actually come off as more butch. . . . But in relationships I've always been more femme. . . . I like femmy butches, and I think I'm a butchy femme." These paradoxical terms do not simply mean "masculine woman"; they are efforts to articulate a complex gendered experience, which our language collapses into two, and only two, categories. Such terms also provide an internal continuity to the various identities that emerge in discrete experiences.

Lesbians cannot fail to be aware that in their choice of women as partners, and in the nontraditional life that accompanies this choice, they defy usual female roles. I think there is always some interplay between masculinity and femininity in lesbianism, not because lesbians are enacting gender roles in conventional ways but because these are the cultural givens. To understand the metapsychological significance of gender and roles in lesbian relationships we need to know the historical-cultural context. What may be meaningful for particular reasons in a particular historical period may be differently understood in later periods. As Katz pointed out, "All homosexuality is situational, influenced and given meaning and character by its location in time and social space" (Katz 1976:7). The same is true of heterosexuality, of course.

Several shifts in the meaning of lesbian gender roles in this century illustrate the necessity of this perspective. Lesbians struggled in the

1920s for public recognition of their relationships. The thinking about homosexuality at the time was determined largely by Havelock Ellis's work, which equated homosexuality with gender inversion. By cross-dressing, these women proclaimed in effect that their relationships were fully sexual ones, not the more acceptable, but asexual, Boston marriage (Newton 1984). They were concerned with establishing their relationships as sexual, not with challenging distortions of gender conceptions. Male homosexual identity was a fairly recent construct, less than a century old. As Elizabeth Wilson writes, "It is not surprising that lesbians, emerging at the same time with a conscious identity, had, during these years, accepted the sexologists' definition of their 'condition' as biologically determined and clinical, one to which masculinity was the key" (1984:215–216).

In the 1950s other concerns were influential. Philip Blumstein and Pepper Schwartz (1983) concluded that "homosexual couples went through the familial fifties along with the rest of the country ... when traditional assumptions about sex roles in marriage remained unchallenged ... many gay and lesbians couples fell into a pattern of role-playing" (1983:44). In other words they saw lesbians as attempting to normalize their relationships by conforming to the conventions of the time in their own way.

By the 1970s feminist and gay liberation movements were critiquing the distortions required by gender rules, arguing that women incorporate supposedly masculine attributes as women, not as men. Proclaiming a masculine identity became questionable; it suggested a devaluation of women. Wilson noted that "the role-playing falsity of gender was, according to this scenario, the mark of heterosexuality, while lesbianism by contrast became the arena for the flowering of real womanhood" (1984:216). Role-playing ceased to be a viable expression of lesbian identity and relationship.

The meaning of gender roles in lesbian relationships continues to evolve as feminist and lesbian movements change their focus. Some lesbians again consider role-playing of a very fluid kind intriguing and erotic. Wendy, a forty-two-year-old white woman raised in a middle-class southern family, was the only woman I interviewed who felt that her relationship incorporated a degree of role-playing. She also revealed a personal "history of identifications."

Over the years I've identified with the terms butch and femme in different ways. Initially it was kind of disgusting to me. . . . I remember reading about role-playing and thinking it was very heterosexual. I didn't understand it except that it was sort of archaic, that it was the way it had been, and it wasn't like that anymore. . . . After coming out and being a lesbian for a while, I took a neutral stance. One of my first girlfriends identified as butch. I had very short hair then and didn't wear makeup or jewelry. I couldn't think of myself as butch exactly, but [laughs] I didn't like the idea of femme, so it was hard to identify with either. . . . I remember when I started wearing make-up or earrings or whatever again. Maybe I put on some lipstick. Now I don't think about it much at all, but I think I would identify as a femme, whatever that means. Some women I've been with feel like they move back and forth, but they identify more as butch. You know [she laughs again], they pack the car and I pack the lunch. . . . I've been with my lover for five years now, and we play around with it. It's fun. We're not role-bound, but we have an acceptance of those ideas [butch and femme], that they're okay, and that they're okay as sexual roles.

Most of the women I talked to made some differentiations about gender between themselves and their partners. It seemed to me that here there was ample room for projection. Because the partners in a lesbian couple may themselves have different conceptions of what each represents in gendered expression, they may make use of it according to their own interests and desires. As some have argued, "In same-sex couples . . . even small differences in the gender identities of the partners might lead them to play different gender roles" (Marecek, Finn, and Cardell 1982:48).

This possibility recalls Winnicott's (1971) concept of potential space, the psychological arena where partners can put their differences (real or imagined) to use. Potential space has been defined as the arena "where meaningful communication takes place. . . . the common ground in affectionate relationships" (Davis and Wallbridge 1981:63). Through psychic play with intimacy and identity, a new creation of self comes into being. As Winnicott wrote:

> The interplay between originality and the acceptance of tradition as the basis for inventiveness seems to me to be just one more example, and a very exciting one, of the interplay between separateness and union. . . . The place where cultural experience is located is in the potential space between the individual and the environment (originally the object). (1971:99–100)

The exchanges that take place in this space provide a kind of complementarity founded on personal conceptions or even fantasies about gender rather than on actual gender-linked behavioral roles. Heterosexual couples may similarly exaggerate gender roles to enhance their sexuality. These interpretations suggest that role-playing is context specific, a form of social and psychological communication. So much constraint is placed upon human development by the demands of gender conformity that unexpressed dimensions of the personality seek new opportunities for appearance here. Again, as Winnicott said, "It is creative apperception more than anything else that makes the individual feel that life is worth living. Contrasted with this is a relationship to external reality which is one of compliance, the world and its details being recognized but only as something to be fitted in with or demanding adaptation" (1971:65).

In their relationships lesbians may draw upon fantasies about what the partner embodies. Complementarity around gender issues sometimes evolves in paradoxical ways. The relationship of Alix and Carol illustrates this point. Alix, forty-three, Jewish, from a working-class background, was married for many years before her involvement with forty-one-year-old Carol, who was raised in a white middle-class Protestant family in the Northeast. When married, Alix had disliked dressing and behaving in typically feminine ways, which she felt objectified her. Now, with a woman, she enjoyed dressing and acting in these same ways. She felt she would not be misunderstood or categorized. She projected onto her lover a familiarity with these things that in fact Carol did not corroborate. At the same time, Alix no longer worried about what she had always considered her more masculine qualities—aggressiveness and ambition—because she assumed they too would be appreciated. I interpret these changes as an expression of an increased sense of subjectivity: looking feminine became an expression of self as subject, with a more self-defined meaning, no longer the object of someone else's meaning. Freed from the confines of conventional gender roles within heterosexual culture, Alix found a personal meaning within her own conceptions of lesbian culture.

Carol shifted, also, toward some traditionally feminine signifiers or attributes: she began wearing more jewelry and she became more emotionally expressive. As she described it, she acquired a defensive sense of emotional invulnerability in her early years as a lesbian, a protective armor against a world that did not value her as she was. Her attachment to this more "masculine" attitude gave way to a greater desire to be expressive and responsive. To her this reflected a revaluing of what was feminine in herself. As Carol and Alix ascribed new meanings to their behavior, appearance, and feelings, various experiences of self opened up correspondingly, which each experienced as a redemption of her feminine self.

Another couple, Miriam, forty-two, and Ellen, thirty-nine, discussed how each had revised her own sense of herself and the other. Miriam was raised in a middle-class urban East Coast Jewish family and Ellen grew up in a white, upper-middle-class suburban California town. Among their many differences, they speculated about their differences in gender positioning. Ellen thought that she had been attracted to Miriam's apparent femininity because it gave her the idea that she would be in control. Instead Miriam turned out to be more often in control, sexually and otherwise. Ellen recognized a femininity in herself through this relationship that surprised her, and they both thought Miriam looked less feminine now. Miriam described a favorite fantasy in which she and Ellen, both in dresses, high heels, and pantyhose, go out to an expensive restaurant. She runs her hand up Ellen's thigh during dinner, realizing how female she is. Miriam says of this fantasy: "This is really lesbian. This is two women. I mean, silky pantyhose and everything. It's a real turn-on—being in a restaurant and sliding my hand under her skirt and over her leg."

Reshaping Genders, Transcending Genders

Suzanne and Abby, both in their mid-thirties and also from very different Jewish and Protestant backgrounds, did not relate to the terms *butch* and *femme* at all. Regarding their appearance, one said: "We can both get very dressed up and be very feminine. We both started wearing makeup after we got together. We can both look like real jocks. We certainly don't use those categories in the way we relate, and we try not to use them sexually."

Wilson (1984) argued that feminism's antagonism to role-playing or lesbian expressions of gender differences denies the potential of homosexuality—its room for psychic play, its capacity for transformation and transcendence of gender. She suggested that "normalizing" lesbianism by denying its use of gender play may itself be homophobic and that feminism has erred in the direction of a new moralism about sexual behavior that emphasizes relationship over sexuality, woman-identification and bonding over eroticized Otherness. Paula spoke about the importance of this kind of psychic play in her life:

I love role stuff. This is one of the things I really love about being lesbian. I love switching roles. . . . There are days I like to look "butch"— wear a leather jacket, look tough. And there are days I like to wear makeup and "femme out." I like both parts of myself, and I have the most latitude to express them as a lesbian. That's true sexually as well.

Homosexuality moves beyond either an affirmation of gender differences or a denial of them. Instead, in Wilson's analysis, it destabilizes our gender conceptions by questioning the construction of gender. This is the threat of homosexuality: "For to insist on lesbianism as a challenge to stereotypes of gender is ultimately . . . political"

(1984:224). It points toward an alternative to institutionalized relationships of domination. Some writers (cf. Dimen 1991; Goldner
1991; Harris 1991) have recognized the potential of conceptualizing
gender as something other than a binary system. We can observe the
presence of this unnamed multiplicity within our culture most visibly in homosexual communities.

The butch has certain psychological functions in the culture. The
way she fails to fit in appears in two guises. In heterosexual and psychoanalytic literature, she appears as the masculine-identified lesbian,
the woman who is not a true woman (McDougall 1980, 1989;
Socarides 1968, 1981). In social terms her marginalized position warns
women of the consequences of failing to be gender appropriate. In
lesbian literature and culture, however, she is otherwise: the strikingly
handsome woman, lonely, aloof, but desirable, romantic, mysterious
(the Byronesque figure depicted by Radclyffe Hall, Colette, Djuna
Barnes, and others [Wilson 1984]). In the first guise she carries cultural fears about gender nonconformity. In the second she holds the
excitement of potentiality (sexual as well as gender).

This second configuration keeps the butch a kind of mythic figure
in lesbian culture. It is the promise she carries that makes lesbians
unwilling to give her up, even where role-playing is not the currency
of the culture. She simultaneously suggests the masterful mother and
the nurturing father. She offers a fortuitous view of what is usually
kept out of sight, the underside of the psyche. This is the excitement
of androgyny—the opportunity it affords for spying beneath the
wraps of social rules.

The figure of the butch redefines the feminine. For lesbians it is
appropriate to speak of differently developed versions of femininity
rather than of masculinity versus femininity. Several women I interviewed broached this idea. Carol articulated it in terms of social power:

It seems to me it's all layers. The more extremely feminine someone is, the more aggressive and power seeking she is, which brings her
around to the other side. It just has to do with . . . how you want to

convey your sense of power to the world. Either extreme, you're try-ing . . . to do that, so it evens out in the end.

Thinking of the feminine this way, as multifaceted experience, is how one comes to understand lesbianism as woman-to-woman love rather than as disguised heterosexual pursuit. The lover seeks the woman in her partner, but it may be a different woman than herself. She seeks the nurturing woman, she seeks the masterful woman, or some less clearly dichotomized femininity, in her lover, and she seeks to know it in herself, in her own grasp of what it is to be female. This is not necessarily the "phallic woman" of psychoanalytic theory, but the woman who does not require the phallus to be empowered, who is empowered by her enhanced experience of what is female.

For many lesbians the choice of another woman as a partner expresses a deep desire not to suffer the constrictions of femininity as mandated in heterosexuality. It is paradoxically a desire to seek within the self a fuller expression of being female or of femininity, if you will. The alternative woman, the woman who spans both ends of the gen-der continuum, is a woman who exists only in the absence of the male. Her lineage goes back to the mythical Greek women who dis-avow marriage and heterosexuality: Athena, Artemis, and Atalanta. Like them, like the "marriage resisters" in China, like women else-where who remain single even when the social cost is high, the les-bian seeks to bring herself into being in a way that seems to be possi-ble in patriarchal cultures only when the male is absent (cf. Raymond 1986; Rich 1980).

The underlying theme that emerged from the interviews was that gen-der is a fluid experience, shifting over time and in the context of one's environment. Through the potential space of conscious and uncon-scious relatedness, a lesbian may use this fluidity to find a place for her-self in the world, to create her own expression of self, and to have it recognized by others. Women draw upon this fluidity in ways that add interest, mystery, and sometimes tension to their intimacy. Their inter-relatedness becomes a medium for adult developmental changes.

I am suggesting that everyone, but perhaps lesbians in particular, has a diversity of gender representations and identifications and that there is usually an unconscious, and sometimes a conscious, oscillation of gender dimensions in lesbian relationships. The gender play might be found along the lines of masculine–feminine complementarity, but it commonly seeks to explore a feminine feminine connection. Not all couples participate in these interactions, and certainly couples who do so do it to different degrees. Though all couples can engage in this kind of exchange, perhaps homosexual couples have both a greater freedom and a greater desire to do so in what are sometimes fairly conscious ways.

Some psychoanalytic writers suggest the potential in heterosexuality for projected and introjected elements of masculinity and femininity between the man and woman (Bergmann 1980; Knight 1940; Murstein 1976). They understand them to strengthen the individual's conventional gender identity: "Feminine wishes in the man and masculine wishes in the woman are projected onto the partner, enhancing one's own gender identity and therefore the boundaries of the self" (Bergmann 1980:74). This kind of exchange may be more important to heterosexual relationships, as these relationships confirm the individual's place within a social institution based upon entrenched gender differences. Between lesbians gender exchanges may expand the woman's sense of gender as well as confirm it. This alternative is also possible heterosexually, of course, but it may be more threatening there.

Perhaps lesbians are not escaping the constraints of femininity into masculinity, or even into androgyny, although that is how many would express it. Instead perhaps they strive to escape some of the limitations of gender categories altogether, into something more variable and fluid, a transcendence of gender rules. These different expressions of gender require us to rethink rigid notions of gender identities as fixed at an early age or as unitary and one-dimensional.

4

Mothers and Daughters in the Family Romance

Although psychoanalytic theory is built upon the significance of family romances—the vicissitudes of love affairs between children and parents—the erotic-romantic aspects of mother-daughter relationships have been neglected. Through decades of elaboration on oedipal triangles within family life, the focus has remained fixed on mother-son and father-daughter concerns. Neglect of the mother-daughter romance is partly a consequence, I think, of overvaluing male development and under-valuing female development. Nevertheless, even feminist analytic writers tend to focus on the attachment and relational aspects of mothers and daughters and touch only minimally on erotic aspects.[1]

In analytic theory identification and rivalry are possible between women, but is anything else? Jessica Benjamin (1988) argues that the traditional view of father-daughter relationships overstresses its import as an erotic relationship and underemphasizes its potential for mutual identification. She does not recognize, however, that the converse is true about the daughter and the mother: their identity is emphasized and their romance is neglected. True to the traditional oedipal para-digm, Ethel Person (1985) states that when a heterosexual woman is in therapy with a woman therapist the transference is one of rivalry, not of erotic feelings. Joyce McDougall (1986) is the rare female analyst to describe a homoerotic countertransference.

This failure to recognize homoerotic transference between women in analysis and psychotherapy mirrors a broader cultural uneasiness with homoerotic elements in mothers' and daughters' ties to each other. With the exception of two recent partnerships of women writers (O'Connor and Ryan 1993; Wrye and Welles 1994), I find none who see this relationship as significant in the way the traditional oedipal relationship is theoretically constructed. Both teams comment on the scant attention in analytic writing to female-female erotic transference. Marginalizing the romantic aspects of mother-daughter love is another way that women's psychological experience is treated as Other within psychoanalysis. Although I am particularly concerned here with how the mother-daughter romance can affect lesbian development, it is also important in heterosexual women's psychology.

Psychoanalytic theory's slight concern with the so-called negative oedipal relationship for both boys and girls—even the naming of it as negative—is unfortunate. Since analytic theory posits that sexual preference comes out of erotic bonds between parents and child, neglecting half of the possibilities there leaves little room to conceptualize homosexuality as something other than failed heterosexuality. Homoerotic desire is in fact usually framed in heterosexual terms—a mimicry of heterosexuality, a failure of heterosexuality, or a distortion of heterosexuality. Psychoanalytic theory discusses homosexuality continually (and pejoratively), but there is usually an assumption that desire is essentially heterosexual. Freud's contention that the question of etiology is equally relevant for both heterosexuality and homosexuality is obscured by the tendency to assume that heterosexuality is normal and natural (cf. Chodorow 1992).

Sexual desire needs to be understood as multidetermined—biological, cultural, and psychodynamic influences converge in the expression of all desire. Both desire and sexual identity need to be understood as more fluid and variable for many individuals than analytic theory tends to recognize. Both Helene Deutsch (1944) and Nancy Chodorow (1978) accepted the bisexual nature of many women's attachments, observing that often the daughter never relinquishes her attachment to the mother even after she extends her desire to the father. Again we are reminded of the story of Persephone. To what degree this attachment includes erotic interests is not clear.

Chapter 2 uses Thomas Ogden's (1987) revision of female sexual development account to suggest a nonpathological pathway toward lesbian development. The daughter emerges from a dyadic relationship with the mother into a triadic one that includes another by using the mother as a transitional object, a potential other. In keeping with Winnicott's (1971) understanding of the paradoxical nature of developmental processes, Ogden sees the mother and daughter as mutually participating in two simultaneous relationships; the old relationship endures even while a newer, more separate one takes the stage. In the newer relationship the mother and daughter have a kind of as-if love affair, a playful transition to an actual third party, with the mother becoming a stand-in for that someone else who will eventually claim the daughter's affections. Since nothing in Ogden's theory depends upon the gender of the third party, the mother may serve as a transition to all other attachments, to other women as well as to men. The mother's success in playing her part does depend, however, according to Ogden, upon her ease in shifting identification from feminine to masculine if she is to mediate her daughter's heterosexuality, or, I would add, her bisexuality. She needs to be comfortable in the "dialectic interplay between masculine and feminine identities" within herself.

Note the assumption here that gender identity is more fluid and varied within the individual than psychoanalytic theory typically recognizes. Expressions of diverse gender identifications by homosexuals are themselves often treated as evidence of pathology. I have suggested that gender expression in lesbians is multilayered, and again I would assert that there is no reason to insist that variations in gender expression are inherently pathological. Perhaps instead it is the rigidity with which polarized gender roles characterize heterosexual culture that is problematic.

Ogden's work suggests that not only does the mother need to have some ease with the interplay between masculinity and femininity in her relationship with her daughter but also with the interplay between heterosexuality and homosexuality. However, both mothers

and fathers may be uncomfortable with this dimension of their relationships with their children. Parents' homophobia, conscious or
unconscious, will undoubtedly affect their interactions and perhaps
skew them away from romantic or erotic elements in them.

This aversion will be responded to by the child in some way. It may
be a determining factor in the child's later object choices, influencing
the sex of the choice. If it doesn't determine the sex, it may still determine gender, so to speak. For example, a woman may prefer extremely
masculine men if she is averse to feminine-feminine connections;
alternately, a woman may prefer a man with feminine qualities if she
is drawn to the feminine but has suppressed it in the course of her
development. It can also influence qualitative aspects of love affairs,
such as a tendency to desire rejecting or devaluing partners. Again,
recalling Benjamin's assertion that the child's fundamental desire is for
recognition, the parents' failure to recognize a child's desire impinges
on the child's developing sense of self, particularly her sexual self and
her gendered self. The effect on lesbian daughters may be different,
however, from the effect on heterosexual daughters.

The paradigm of the so-called negative oedipal relationship posits
that the daughter identifies with the father and loves the mother.
Benjamin writes that all daughters need to identify with their fathers
and need recognition of this identity from their fathers. This identification is not necessarily founded on gender, however. The daughter's
gender identity may still be established through her continuing simultaneous identification with her mother. She can identify with her father
as Other, as separate from mother but still related. She can see herself as
like him, autonomously and actively loving mother, along with many
other qualities about him. A mother's female lover can serve the same
identificatory role. The daughter can claim some of the rights and priv-
ileges of the Other because they are not seen as exclusively male.

She can identify with the father in this way if the family tolerates
it, as families sometimes do. When this identification is denied, some
attribute must be found to account for this failure. Then she may
understand gender as the relevant variable; then she may conclude that
being male is so unlike being female that no identification is possible.

Accepting these possibilities turns some fundamental tenets of psychoanalytic theory around. As Noreen O'Connor and Joanna Ryan (1993) note, psychoanalytic theory treats what one wants to be (identification) as mutually exclusive with what one wants to have (object choice). Nevertheless, both McDougall (1986) and Benjamin (1988) have argued that children do want to be and to have both parents. McDougall treats this as an impossibility that must be given up on the road to maturity, while Benjamin argues that the inability to identify with both parents is a developmental calamity. She does not explore, however, the consequences of thwarted homoerotic desire.

Our understanding of the scope of the mother-child romance needs to be broadened. It is often treated as a developmental event, a phase-specific aspect of early childhood. The erotic bond between child and mother begins in early infancy and is a mutual affair, not just a developmental phase for the child. The mother's passionate attraction and attachment to the child ensures her devoted attention, her admiration of every detail of the child's being, and is essential to the child's development. Unless we restrict eroticism to a strictly genital experience, we see that the mother-infant relationship, grounded in physical, sensual contact, in pleasure and satisfaction, is erotic from the beginning.

A sharp theoretical distinction is made between preoedipal and oedipal eroticism, with the latter being more genitally focused. This distinction may be more relevant to male development than female. Nevertheless there is a shift for the daughter as well, and the oneness with mother gives way to a greater degree of separateness from her. As this happens, the daughter too may begin to court the mother, to woo her across the space that is opening between them. This courtship may be erotically charged without being as genitally focused as the boy's. Likewise adult women's sexuality often does not reflect the genital preoccupation of male sexuality and is likely to be tied inextricably to emotional and sensual experiences in which genital sexuality is only one part. Elements of the daughter's courtship and the mother's response may reappear in psychotherapy with adult women in the transference.

When all is well parents dote on their children; it is an attraction like no other. The attraction between mother and daughter continues throughout development, altering in form and intensity but nevertheless persisting. This attraction deserves recognition in its shifting forms. We can locate it in adult relationships between women, in friendships as well as in sexual relationships. If the mother fails to feel this attraction or subverts it in some way, there are consequences for the child. And, again, when the daughter's own desires are oriented primarily toward women, this rejection or neglect will be especially significant.

The therapeutic dangers in erotic transference and countertransference are well described in the psychoanalytic literature.[2] These feelings may defend against other feelings or serve to resist the therapy, they can be unmanageable and end the therapy, or they can be a crucial source of insight and transformation. Even though erotic feelings are understood to be pleasurable, in therapy they are usually realized with dread by both client and therapist (Kumin 1985). I describe two cases here as examples of erotic transference that require the therapist to recognize the emergence of these feelings and to tolerate the complexity of her own responses. In these cases the erotic feelings remained covert or were hidden for a long time, presenting a different dilemma than more overt desires that patients sometimes feel. The latter present an undeniable therapeutic issue for both therapist and patient, but a more covert experience may be missed or dismissed as unimportant. In both situations, however, the risk lies in "analyzing away" such transferences, simply reenacting the maternal relationship.

I describe one clinical experience with a lesbian client and one with a heterosexual client, to avoid the tendency to dichotomize homosexual and heterosexual development into two utterly distinct categories, a tendency that has been part of the theoretical misunderstanding of both sexuality and gender. Both cases were long-term therapies with a woman therapist and involved many issues, but I have focused only on aspects relevant to erotic transference and countertransference. The first case is more detailed because I am primarily concerned with lesbian development here.

Desire Within the Transference: A Lesbian Patient

The therapeutic work with a woman I'll call Joanne illustrates one way that difficulties with erotic/romantic feelings in a mother-daughter relationship later create problems for the daughter. Joanne, a Jewish woman in her mid-forties who was raised in the Northeast, was in therapy to deal with pervasive feelings of unhappiness. A successful physician, she had had an unhappy six-year marriage and was in a relatively happy ten-year relationship with another woman. Although she experienced both love and desire with men, she felt she was always more interested in a relationship with a woman and considered herself to be lesbian.

She loved and felt loved by Dede, her partner, but the sexual aspect of their relationship had diminished, and Joanne suffered a profound sense of aloneness. She was plagued by depression and by feeling that there was something fundamentally wrong with herself. A great deal of the work revolved around her effort to feel a genuine sense of contact with the therapist. In the beginning she valued the sessions strictly according to how much contact she felt she had made. What she really needed from her therapist, she said, was for her to care about her personally in a way that she probably never could. She kept this desire vague and disavowed sexual interests or feelings for a long time. The thought of such feelings frightened her considerably.

Talking about her wish for the therapist to care for her personally was difficult because she believed the therapist might actually send her away in response. When she first had dreams that suggested romantic/sexual encounters between herself and someone who might represent the therapist, she found little to say about them. The therapist occasionally showed up in her dreams in a sexually neutral guise, but if ever there were a suggestion of sexuality between them, there was danger. For example, once she dreamed they were looking at each other in a quasi-sexual way and an earthquake struck.

Joanne began to be much concerned with gender issues. She revealed that she did not really identify herself as either feminine or masculine. A recurring dream was not being able to find anything to wear that fit her. For example, she would find herself in a dress and high heels, clothes that felt extremely uncomfortable to her. In her closet there would be no other clothes or only clothes that were even more uncomfortable, such as a man's suit. The clothes she actually wore were nonspecific for gender. The degree to which she felt alienated from things identified as either feminine or masculine troubled her because it signified to her that she did not fit anywhere. The theme of recognition, both by herself and others, was very important in her work.

Joanne also focused on her feelings about her father, with whom she had an ambivalent relationship. She identified with him in ways she was reluctant to recognize, partly because he embodied qualities she disliked and considered masculine, especially his aggressiveness. She had a series of dreams about dirty bathrooms, which, because they were so dirty, she refused to use. In these dreams she was inevitably trapped—there was no other bathroom and she had a great need for one. She linked these dreams to her relationship with her father, who seemed to her to be a dirty necessity since she had an even more estranged relationship with her mother. She sensed the possibility of a sexual meaning to these dreams but did not explore it further.

Joanne's mother epitomized East Coast propriety. She was functionally adequate but emotionally distant and disapproving, especially about Joanne's lesbianism. Joanne had given up hope of closer family relationships and rarely visited her parents. She assumed them to be equally relieved to avoid her, even though they continued to try to get her to come for family occasions and holidays.

Some of her dreams concerned a high school teacher she had adored, a woman who was both kind and distant with her. She described herself as having been infatuated with this woman in a hopeless, unrequited way. The emergence of the beloved teacher in her awareness brought the issue of her love and desire for other women back to an uncomfortable place. This sense of her desire as inappropriate, as utterly unacceptable, and as something that must somehow be eliminated (as in the need for a bathroom) was pervasive. One dream several months after the therapist returned from a maternity leave particularly helped to focus Joanne's feelings about her.

In this dream she was on a trip with her therapist, staying overnight in a dormitory-style room. Other people were there, and she had to sleep in the same bed as the therapist. During the night she put her hand on the therapist's leg and the therapist got very upset with her. Joanne got out of bed, walked around, and came back again, lying very still in an effort not to touch. She was troubled, however, about how she was supposed to sleep in the same bed without touching. The next morning in the dream they were waiting for an elevator. Now the therapist was a mother, holding her baby. A little four-year-old girl was there also. This child had not done a very good job of wiping herself in the bathroom and was covered with shit. Joanne, watching her, wanted to take the little girl to the bathroom and clean her up so she wouldn't be so disgusting to everyone.

This dream helped Joanne to crystallize certain feelings she had about mothers and daughters and therapists and patients. Babies were lovable, she thought, in a way that four-year-old girls were not. Therapists were like mothers, happy to be nurturing and tending a baby, but they—both therapists and mothers—were offended by an older child's touch, by desire, which is not unlike shit. Nevertheless, she could not understand how two people could be close enough to sleep in the same bed and never touch. It seemed natural to her that they would touch. She could not resolve this dilemma. The dream left her hopeless, feeling powerless and lost. The only possible action was that of cleaning up the little girl.

Joanne's conscious feelings toward the therapist continued to be strong but sexually muted. Equally important were the therapist's own responses. She was uncomfortable about the attraction and desire toward her that Joanne's work indicated. She didn't welcome such feelings. Paying more attention to her feelings and relating them to the therapy, she realized her countertransference was a significant part of Joanne's unconscious experience with her: the negative feelings replicated something in Joanne's experience. These feelings would more or less dissolve after the therapist acknowledged them to herself and considered their countertransferential meaning—only to return later for another round. Both Joanne's and the therapist's mutual discomfort with Joanne's potential for sexual and romantic interest in the therapist became the therapeutic ground of their relationship.

Joanne's desire was felt and expressed primarily in terms of her love for the therapist and of her wish for her to love her in return. That is, it was felt and expressed as an emotional desire more than as a physical, sexual one. Again, I think this emphasis is not uncommon for women, who may experience desire in romantic more than erotic terms. But it also represents the neutralizing of homoerotic love, which has been experienced as threatening to the relationship. It was important not to miss or minimize the erotic aspect of her desire, even where it was more implicit than explicit.

The therapist understood, perhaps in a different way than Joanne did, that Joanne needed her to have a positive emotional response to her barely expressed sexual feelings for her—to see her as a desirable woman and also to recognize and be pleased by her love and desire for Dede. In the grips of the most feared part of these feelings, Joanne began an intense and passionate flirtation with another woman. With some interpretive help she came to realize that the new flirtation was a displacement of feelings that felt too dangerous elsewhere.

As the therapist came to support and then welcome the emergence of Joanne's love and of her erotic self, Joanne began to find parts of her identity and her emotional life that had been lost or undeveloped. This work was not always explicit, as Joanne would perhaps have fled from therapy if it had been otherwise. Further, since the therapist carried Joanne's projection of the mother who could not respond to her daughter's desire, it was a matter for the therapist to recognize and process silently. Eventually they were able to construct together an understanding of Joanne's relationship with her mother that included this knowledge, but they did not explore the therapist's complementary response. In this sense the therapy is not unlike the mother-daughter relationship, in which such feelings may be welcomed by the mother, but the mother does not speak directly about them—and perhaps does not even need to be conscious of them. In fact, to speak about them would be overwhelming and confusing to the child. To be very conscious of them might constrict the

mother. This exchange is important at an unconscious level as much
as a conscious one.

Joanne's growing awareness of the interpersonal dimension of her
internal responses led to a narrative framework that allowed her to
understand herself in a new way. The therapist's participation in
developing this narrative was both interpretive and responsive—
reflecting with her on the significance and authenticity of Joanne's
account. Joanne came to life within this reflection and repeatedly let
the therapist know how important the therapist's "seeing" her was.
Joanne's mother was both depressed and severely emotionally restricted. Her love for her child was expressed largely through physical caretaking, with an emphasis on keeping her clean and protecting her
physical safety. She was unresponsive to Joanne's emotional overtures
and probably appalled by her daughter's passionate feelings.

When she began therapy Joanne's story of her relationship with her
mother was that she, Joanne, had rejected her mother. She loved the
mothers of her friends more than her own mother and sought them
out all through her childhood. In the therapy Joanne developed a different story about her childhood. In this version her rejection of her
mother was secondary, a defensive response to feeling rejected by her
mother. The evidence for this story lay primarily in her enormous
fear of rejection by the therapist. She believed that if she deeply loved
or desired someone, these feelings alone would cause the other to
reject her. The therapist's initial discomfort with her desire to be loved
constituted this rejection and allowed her to silently confirm the truth
of Joanne's developing narrative.

In the new story her relationship with her father was also contam-
inated by the mother's rejection. He was the consolation prize, sullied
by a child's desire that had been revealed to be dirty. She could "elim-
inate" her sexual feelings by directing them toward him or, later,
toward other men, but it was not her true desire. Their relationship
was further troubled by Joanne's envy of his access to the mother and
her feelings of competitiveness with him, as her mother seemed to
prefer her husband to her daughter. These emotions made it difficult
to love her father unambivalently.

Her father had actually been more responsive to her in many ways than her mother. She identified with him as one who preferred an active mode. Rather than disapproving of her "tomboyishness," as she called it, like her mother did, her father enjoyed it. She remembered now how much she had enjoyed being outdoors, fishing, playing ball, going on his work rounds with him rather than being trapped in the confines of her mother's neat house. Eventually this work led Joanne to see that her defensive rejection of her mother had in turn led her mother to be even more distant with her. This allowed her to grasp their situation as mutually painful, not simply as one in which she was the victim. She began to make some guarded overtures to her mother and to consider a brief family visit.

Joanne's work on her relationship with her mother and her some-what parallel one with the therapist shifted her gendered sense of self. For the first time she had dreams of clothes she liked to wear. They were women's clothes but unconstricting. Once she dreamed that she wore a suit tailored out of a beautiful fabric made especially for her. She felt very good wearing this suit. There were other, subsequent dreams in which she again couldn't find the right thing to wear, but now there were more choices and usually she could find something she could accept. She felt that she had become gender "suitable."

Joanne's gender "suitability" emerged in the context of her relationship with the therapist, partly through a new sense of identification with another woman. Perhaps equally important, however, she felt that the therapist accepted and recognized her womanliness, not wanting her to be different, not requiring her to be the same kind of woman she was. Initially she had the idea that her mother had wanted her to be a boy, that her mother's rejecting feelings were a response to Joanne's gender. Later she decided that her mother had preferred Joanne's friends, who were more feminine. The problem was not that she was a girl but that she was not girlish enough. It was her version of femininity that her mother had rejected, she thought, because it wasn't the conventional one.

Joanne experienced her homosexuality as inborn, as having always been true for her. She thought her unconventionality as a girl was indicative of this. Whether these two things are necessarily associated, Joanne experienced them as intrinsically associated within herself. This led her and the therapist to understand the hopelessness of her dilemma. When she wooed her mother as a girl, she failed, because she was a girl. Her mother could not engage with her daughter in an as-if relationship while recognizing her femininity. At the same time, when Joanne wooed her mother as an as-if boy, she failed, because she was boyish, which her mother rejected as well.

Her mother, uncomfortable with blurring the boundaries between masculinity and femininity, between homosexuality and heterosexuality, could not respond positively to a daughter who desired to play with her romantically. She could only be a suitor if she were not a girl; she could only be a girl if she were not a suitor. This was a dilemma Joanne could not solve except by diminishing significant aspects of herself. Perhaps her friends, more heterosexually inclined and more traditionally feminine, did not press her mother into difficult choices that led to rejection. In other words, perhaps they were more like the mother herself.

To some degree her wounded sense of femaleness was helped by her relationship with Dede, who welcomed Joanne's nontraditional femininity. Further reparation came within the transference: she felt recognized as a woman and as a woman of desire. The child's dilemma of irreparable unsuitability was relieved at last: the internal rejecting mother was modified by an internalized welcoming maternal presence who found her essentially suitable. In relationship to both Dede and the therapist, although in different ways, she could be a woman involved authentically with another woman, not in a skewed attempt at indirect heterosexuality. The recognition of both her femaleness and her desire was the crucial therapeutic experience.

Toward the end of therapy Joanne dreamed she encountered the therapist teaching a physics class. As teacher, her method was playful, which was disturbing to some in the class but not to Joanne. The therapist/teacher danced around the classroom and invited Joanne to dance with her, but Joanne was too shy and could only extend her arms. Then they were together elsewhere and making out passionately. The experience was very sexual, very mutual, and made Joanne happy. It occurred to her that maybe it did not mean as much to the therapist as it did to herself—maybe she was still being playful, while Joanne was willing to leave Dede. She realized leaving Dede would be a mistake, and she was also worried about how this would affect the therapy. This problem remained unresolved at the end of the dream, but she woke up happy.

This dream was extremely meaningful to her because she felt fully sexual in the dream as she had not for a long time. The mutuality of the passion was more important than the dangers in their encounter and her willingness to take the risks and tolerate what was unresolved in the dream pleased her. She was happy with the dream, with her sense of aliveness in it, and happy to tell the therapist about it, expecting her to understand and share her good feelings. The therapist was teaching a physics class, and, because physics is related to her field, she believed she was speaking her language. I note also that it is the language of physical things, i.e., perhaps bodily things.

Desire Within the Transference: A Heterosexual Patient

The second woman, Susan, was also in her mid-forties. An Asian-American woman raised in a wealthy Pacific Northwestern family, she came to therapy for help with depression and a sense of isolation that persisted in spite of a good marriage and family life and a career as a professional musician. Questions about her sexuality were not part of the therapy. Compared to Joanne, Susan more traditionally identified as feminine. She was disturbed, however, by a sense of falseness about herself that she saw in terms of gender. She felt that she constructed her own femininity, that it was not genuine. She did not identify with her mother, whom she largely rejected.

Susan described her mother as extremely feminine—that is, beautiful, childlike, and fairly incompetent in the world. Susan felt loved by her mother but also felt they had some early parting of the ways she could not explain, something unnamed that didn't work well between them. Like Joanne's, Susan's mother was critical and preoccupied with propriety. She idealized men to the detriment of herself and other women. Susan was aware that she was like her mother in many ways. She, too, was critical and plagued by propriety, even while she rebelled against it. She also presented herself as somewhat childlike or girlish: cute, coy—even petulant—and naive. She recognized this self as false, but considered her more adult qualities masculine.

Susan idealized her father, as her mother did, and identified with him in important ways, but this identity also lacked authenticity for her. It allowed her to appear self-confident even though her self-esteem was low. She thought of it as armor that she could put on and take off. Her gendered self thus felt false, and her emotional life was limited by these gender issues. Emotionality was associated with her mother, whom she rejected; she correspondingly rejected and disparaged her own emotional experience.

Only in her career as a musician did she transcend this dilemma. In the creative realm, she found, gender did not exist. In one session she described how she did not identify with her name when friends used it. Her self had no name; it had no gender, it was an "it." No one could know or name this self because the self would then be required to conform to the other's will. She rarely told dreams, even though she remembered many dreams. Dreams were part of her private self, which she was not ready to expose or explore. She found therapy painful and unpleasant and compared it to childbirth. She hoped it would be over fast.

In the transference it became clear that she was not only afraid of being controlled by others if she revealed her true self, she was even more afraid of rejection. Women were especially dangerous in this regard, and she was slow to trust the therapist. She equated the end of therapy with being abandoned by her, proving that the therapist had not cared about her authentically. She wondered if they might be friends afterward. At the same time, she frequently devalued the therapist, her office, and the therapy.

When the therapist was late for one session, she assumed she had been called home for an emergency with her child and she said she was thrilled to have therapy canceled. This was also her response to vacations, holidays, or absences. She saw how her devaluing of the therapist could protect her, but she did not believe her feelings were defensive. When the therapist suggested that Susan's idea of the therapist's rushing home to take care of a child had made Susan feel diminished—less of a priority—Susan became very sad and talked about how her mother did not value her. She said she could not bear that again with anyone.

Sometimes Susan related to the therapist flirtatiously, making her appeal in small, stereotypically feminine, ways, being charming, being coy. Occasionally she made subtly alluring gestures or sat in provocative poses. There was a hopeful quality to this behavior, much like a little girl trying to discover where her powers of attraction might be. Her awareness of the meaning of this behavior was limited to a safely conventional one. When the therapist noted the coyness in her behavior, she quickly identified it as part of her little-girl heterosexuality, behavior she learned from her mother and employed with her father. When the therapist pointed out that she used it with her too, she said that the therapist was a professional and an authority figure and therefore like her father.

Her interpretation was accurate but, nevertheless, defensive because it omitted another aspect of their relationship—her fantasy of having a more intimate relationship with a woman. She talked about other women constantly: they were clearly central to her psychic life. She longed for women to be close with. Even though she had many friends, she was not really close to anyone other than her husband. She complained that he was not enough, that she needed intimacy with a woman in some way. The childlike quality of her appeal to the therapist suggested that they were dealing with deeply submerged remnants of her courtship of her mother and subsequent rejection.

Susan was appealing, but the therapist felt anxious about her flirtatiousness and her desire to know her outside therapy. Further, she sensed a readiness on Susan's part to reject her. Periodically she felt uncomfortable with the intensity of Susan's efforts to engage her and was put off by her girlishness. At the same time, it was important that the therapist recognize her as a woman of ability and competence. The dialectic tension between these aspects of herself was always present. The painful meaning embedded in this behavior, both the rejected desire and the sense of unworthiness, disturbed the therapist. Again, the therapist's recognition of her own feelings and their meaning in the therapy was a turning point. Acceptance of Susan's longing for intimacy with a woman, conveyed in this anxious way through the therapy, was essential. Romantic aspects of this longing were real and required implicit, more than explicit, recognition.

Susan's mother, who valued men over women, could not respond fully or positively to her young daughter's longing to be valued and loved as female, by a female. Further, the mother's own sense of self was weak and a vacuous version of adult femininity was all she could offer her daughter for identification. Susan constructed, as she put it, a self to manage the situation, but it did not feel like a self with substance. Her lack of authenticity was not related solely to the problematics of gender, but significant elements of it were, and these elements have traditionally been underrecognized in women's development.

At one point in the therapy the therapist dreamed about Susan the night before a session with her. In this dream Susan invited the therapist into her (current) family. Contrary to the therapist's expectations, she discovered that she felt comfortable there. In the session the next day Susan talked about how often she was surprised in therapy by what she said and felt. Then she blurted out that she couldn't trust that the therapist cared about her because she was not "in her face," as she put it, with assurances of valuing her. As the session progressed, the therapist saw her own young daughter's face superimposed on Susan's. She didn't discuss the dream or this odd experience with Susan, but the session indicated to her that they had struggled through the distrust and threat of intimacy to at least a momentary state of mutuality. They had allowed each other to participate in their familial ties in acknowledgment of their unconscious relationship.

Cultural and Psychological Dimensions of the Mother-Daughter Romance

Psychoanalytic theory has constructed femininity, and gender identity in general, in strictly heterosexual terms. The daughter's femininity is established solely through identification with the mother and desire for the father. The reverse can only mean trouble: identification with the father is a pathological masculine identification and desire for the mother is either defense against failure in heterosexuality or regressive fusion with the mother. Joyce McDougall (1980 and 1989), in her writings about lesbians, understands femininity essentially and exclusively in terms of heterosexuality. Her work implicitly assumes that a woman's lesbianism itself establishes a distortion in her gender identity. In general, psychoanalysis credits the father-daughter relationship with influencing the daughter's sexual and gender esteem or how a woman feels about herself as female and as sexual (Leonard 1966).

As O'Connor and Ryan point out, the possibility for a woman to feel "more securely and positively female" through relationships with other women "is missing from conventional psychoanalytic accounts, where femininity can only ever be realised through heterosexual engagement" (1993:129). Since femininity is gained only through relationship and intercourse with a man, clinical accounts of lesbians treat this other possibility as fantasy or illusion, evidence of the denial of reality that homosexuality supposedly represents. These presumptions about gender and object choice rest upon dualistic and complementarity conceptions of gender identities (i.e., one is established as female by not being what the male is) and the construction of gender in terms of heterosexuality (i.e., if one loves a woman, one is masculine).

From my perspective, with women (especially Other women) in the center of the story, the mother-daughter romance plays a significant role for all women and a potentially crucial one for lesbians. While I believe that evidence of this in clinical practice is common, we tend to theorize primarily about the risks within this relationship. Again, quoting O'Connor and Ryan, the problem lies in the notion "that the relationship with the mother is always and inevitably something to be avoided and only grown away from, rather than explored and changed in various adult forms" (271). The psychoanalytic assumption that identifications and object choice are necessarily split according to gender, the cornerstone of oedipal theory, cannot be empirically or clinically substantiated. We know otherwise from the experience of transference in which identification and object choice can readily alternate, where both client and therapist imaginatively shift their relationship. Here we experience with some awareness the way in which identifications are imaginal acts with great potential for fluidity.

Why have we found this awareness so difficult and so late in coming? The fault lies at least in part with the failure of psychoanalysis to consider its own dread of sexual and gender variation as well as its patriarchal assumptions that privilege the phallus as representative of entry into the world of language, reason, otherness, and maturity. As feminist and postmodern perspectives influence psychoanalytic thinking, we can see these constructions in a different way.

For female development to reach its fullest expression, there must be a strong positive sense of female relationship that is not concerned with the male/father, one in which women are not rivals for the desired object but are desired and desiring themselves in relation to each other, as Other. This possibility does not preclude relationship with the male/father, but may coexist with it, as in the story of Persephone. The female relationship does not come to an end with the beginning of relationship with the father but has its own continuing developmental life. If this relationship is weak, or if it is weakened by an absence of passionate feeling, then some degree of a sense of authenticity and adequacy is lost. If there is not some sense of the mother and daughter finding each other whole and complete without this sense coming through the male, then the daughter may have difficulty feeling subjectively whole within herself.

To facilitate the daughter's sense of authenticity and subjectivity—sexual and otherwise—the mother must be, as Benjamin has well described, a sexual subject herself, not simply a sexual object. She must have her own sense of agency rather than seeking it through a man's. The mother cannot recognize and reflect the fullness of her daughter's being without possession of her own. Just as with the father, the reluctance or inability of the mother to participate in this relationship may be incorporated by the daughter as a reflection of her undesirability, as a lack in her sexual, gendered self. Further, when a mother's inhibition or rejection of a daughter's desire is based on homophobia, the failure occurs precisely because of the daughter's gender. The gender-determined basis of this response seems to be communicated to the daughter.

Mothers, like fathers, dealing with a child's passionate feelings, may be responsive within the unconscious relationship they have with their children even when they are not comfortable with awareness of its meaning. Capacity for responsiveness to the mother-daughter love affair depends in part on the quality of the mother's relationship with her own mother, or on reparations she has made to the wounds of that relationship, rather than on awareness of the emotional dynamics between mothers and daughters.

The mother's homophobic response, as well as her own construction of gender, are influenced by time and place. Whenever sexuality and gender are discussed, both cultural and dynamic analyses need to remain in view as far as possible. What Susan thinks of as masculine in herself, her sense of competence and maturity, she cannot fully claim, in part because the terms of culturally dictated heterosexuality do not allow it. These qualities belong exclusively to men. Structurally, the heterosexuality of our culture is about masculinity and femininity in a more or less traditional sense. Altering those terms would border on homosexuality, unconsciously speaking. Susan's internalization of her mother's rejection of her courtship makes even this symbolic version of homosexuality difficult for her.

The lesbian daughter's incorporation of the mother's discomfort complicates her efforts to understand her sexuality in positive terms. This early failure is compounded again when the adult daughter comes out to her mother and receives a negative response. Difficulties are not confined to sexual relationships. Some women fear getting close to other women even in nonsexual relationships. Many women carry a fear of rejection in relation to other women: they expect their loving feelings to be disturbing to each other and therefore suppress or counteract them with other feelings. Women, as friends or as lovers, often feel a great sense of vulnerability with each other. They already know what rejection by another woman feels like, even when they do not connect these feelings to their mothers.

I agree with some feminist writers that women tend to be more oriented toward intimacy in relationships of all kinds and that the boundary between sexual and nonsexual desires can be indistinct. Both Chodorow's (1978) and Benjamin's (1988) work, as well as the work of the Stone Center (a group of feminist clinicans and theorists at Wellesley college [Jordan et al. 1991]), emphasize the relational grounds of woman's sexual self. Since women's sexual desires often represent a desire for closeness (while the opposite may be true more often of men), the confusion between loving and sexual feelings is understandable. At the same time, lesbians may convert sexual desires exclusively into desire for closeness of a nonsexual kind. This loss of desire can be understood in part as a response to the experience of emotional danger vis-à-vis sexual desire.

Some women acquire a sense of sexual agency through identification with the father. This was true for both Joanne and Susan, to some extent, but, for each, other aspects of themselves felt acquired rather than intrinsic. In a culture where genders are deeply polarized categories, it can be problematic in various ways for the daughter to identify with the father. Further, for these two women, their particular fathers were not unproblematic within the family, increasing the discomfort with their identification. Both wanted a sense of agency through the female self. Both experienced this most fully in a therapy where the male/father was not present.

While one came to therapy with a weak sense of her own feminine identity and the other had a more stereotypical one, both felt fundamentally alienated from a gendered sense of self. We live in a cultural era that is tentatively accepting a broader view of sexuality and gender, one that acknowledges more diversity in both than social or psychological theories have previously sanctioned. We are beginning to

understand that sexuality and gender cannot be adequately understood in terms of dichotomies or exclusive categories. Neither is well
defined by a binary system. These social changes may influence family relationships in various ways. For many women these changes also
contribute to reparation of the wounds to their esteem. The therapist's
awareness of these dimensions of female experience is necessary for
psychotherapy to be part of this reparation rather than a reenactment
of this kind of rejection.

PART TWO

Families of Women

5

Themes in Lesbian Relationships: The Question of Merger

The first studies of lesbian relationships appeared in the work of sexologists like Richard von Krafft-Ebing (1886) and Havelock Ellis (1928). Ellis's observations reflected the prevailing view at the time: a strong belief in a natural gender polarization in relationships. Like Krafft-Ebing, he determined that lesbianism was actually gender inversion, i.e., a masculine personality within a feminine body. Lesbian relationships, they thought, involved one somewhat masculine woman (the "active invert") partnered with a more feminine woman, who was perhaps lesbian only by default, having been influenced or seduced by the other. Subsequent studies of lesbian couples were thereafter primarily interested in the phenomenon of role-playing, until the feminist influence of the 1970s offered another view. Psychoanalytic studies were also influenced by this work and tended to analyze couples first in terms of gender roles and only secondarily using other parameters.

By the 1960s psychoanalysis had firmly fixed lesbian relationships in one stage or another of dire pathology. For example, Charles Socarides (1968) wrote that lesbian relationships are characterized by "hate, destructiveness, mutual defeat, exploitation of the partner and the self, oral-sadistic incorporation, aggressive onslaughts, attempts to alleviate anxiety and a pseudo-solution to the aggressive and libidinal urges which dominate and torment the individual." Joyce McDougall

(1980) similarly stated that analysis of lesbian relationships "invariably reveals the greedy, destructive and manipulatory anal-controlling aspects of the relationship." These accounts read like indictments, not dispassionate analyses.

By far the majority of recent work on lesbian couples lies outside the psychoanalytic domain and is undertaken from the perspective of social psychology, sociology, or feminism. Current studies, usually based on empirical research, create a picture of lesbian couples which, if nothing else, refutes that dire portrait of unhappiness offered by the more extreme psychoanalysts. They also alter the picture of a lesbian couple from one that mimics the masculine/feminine roles of hetero-sexual couples to one with different values. Much research explores whether lesbians are satisfied in their relationships or, comparatively, whether lesbians are more or less satisfied than heterosexual or gay male couples. In these studies lesbians as a group are just as happy with their relationships as other kinds of couples.[1]

Further information from these studies gives a rough profile of les-bian couples. Lesbians desire and find a high degree of intimacy in their relationships. Lesbian couples value equality more than other kinds of partners, and they develop greater mutuality in decision mak-ing and in handling household and other tasks. Lesbians' partners have more in common in certain key dimensions—their demographic characteristics are more similar, their relationship values more closely approximate each other's, and their feelings of love for each other more nearly match. They desire and spend more time together than other kinds of partners do.

Lesbian couples are more affectionate and sensual with each other. Apparently lesbians have sex less frequently but are more responsive and more satisfied than heterosexual women are with the sex that they do have (Blumstein and Schwartz 1983; Loulan 1988). The complex issue of sexuality for women in general and in lesbian relationships is the subject of chapter 7.

Some data suggest that lesbian relationships don't last as long as het-erosexual ones (Tanner 1978). Assertions about longevity are haz-ardously made, however, because many lesbians have gone through a change of identity and choice of sexual partners well beyond adolescence. Their relationships reflect the turmoil of these changes. If comparisons are to be made between lesbians and heterosexuals, midlife relationships would be a more reliable baseline. It is also problematic to make comparisons when one of the compared populations is a relatively hidden one. We have no way of knowing, for example, how many covert long-term relationships exist. There is also the problem of how fast the picture is changing for heterosexual couples as well, now that the social bonds that have sustained them are shifting.

These studies answer basic questions about the nature of lesbian relationships and put lesbian couples on the map, in terms of research. By their nature as quantitative studies, however, they are limited. More subtle, more individual, and more unconscious dynamics of intimate relating are left to qualitative studies, clinical accounts, and theoretical analyses, a small number of which do formulate a dynamic understanding of lesbians in couples. Taken together, empirical and theoretical approaches suggest several broad themes that characterize lesbian couples. To interpret their meaning in lesbian psychology, these themes need to be grounded in their historical and social context and related to all feminine psychology. By placing Other women (lesbian, bisexual, and heterosexual) in the center of this account and extrapolating from their experience, the narrative themes we detect here are open to normative interpretations. These interpretations are then relevant to broad groups of women, further challenging the categorical distinction between lesbians and heterosexual women.

Friendship, closeness, and emotional attachment is the first theme. One might expect this to be a beginning point for all couples, but distinctions between lesbian couples and friendships have a curious history that sets them apart from other kinds of relationships. A second theme is the question of psychological merger and personal autonomy. The theme of merger is related to the theme of attachment and intimacy but has another dimension to it, the loss of individual boundaries. Attachment and autonomy are not mutually exclusive, but merger and autonomy sometimes are. A third issue, taken up in the next chapter, is the balance of power between lesbian partners. The effort to maintain equality often becomes a dominant concern between women, and this effort can be viewed from several perspectives.

Friendship, Closeness, and Attachment

The distinction between friends and lovers seems to be less clear between lesbians than between heterosexuals. Historically, the distinction was often collapsed altogether: in terms of social awareness, women were never considered to be more than friends, but the intensity of their friendship might surpass the intimacy of any other relationship in their lives. In recent times some feminists have placed all significant relationships between women on a "lesbian continuum," and thus they have completely blurred the distinction between friends and lovers (Rich 1980; Raymond 1986). Some contemporary studies of lesbian relationships also show that boundaries between friends and lovers are blurred in a variety of ways.

In past centuries female couples (we can hardly call them lesbians, a conception not in existence over a hundred years ago) occupied an ambiguous social position. Some partnerships between women, many of them lifelong, enjoyed a very high degree of social recognition on the assumption that they were nonsexual.[2] Referred to sometimes as *passionate friendships,* sometimes as *Boston marriages,* they allowed women a legitimized intimacy in an era when intimate relationships between men were harshly penalized because their sexual nature was acknowledged. These relationships existed between women who were married to men as well as between women who lived with each other. The evidence of their passion is found in love letters preserved by families as well as in oral and other written traditions. They testify to relationships in which women slept with each other (sometimes replacing the husband in the marital bed for extended periods), frequently caressed and kissed each other, but perhaps were never explicitly sexual, at least as sexual is defined heterosexually (Smith-Rosenberg 1975). The work of Ellis and Krafft-Ebing altered the public image of female couples; it broke the denial of sexuality between women. Passionate friendships as a social institution began appearing suspect and public discourse then rallied against them (Faderman 1991).

The notion that deep and intimate friendship is the primary bond between women in relationships continues. Many lesbians consider their lover their closest friend and find it quite difficult to distinguish between the words *lover* and *friend,* finally relying on sexual activity as the only distinction (Vetere 1982). One writer argues that the relationship model characterizing lesbian relationships is not that of heterosexual couples, but of best friends, with the added element of romantic attraction (Peplau 1981). Relationships between lesbian ex-lovers underscores the central role of friendship and attachment in lesbian relationships. Ex-lovers often become a kind of extended family for lesbians, and many women devote enormous effort to the transition from lover to friend once the couple relationship ends. These continuing ties may interfere with forming new relationships, but they also enrich the sense of connection and community, supplementing and sometimes replacing what families of origin provide to heterosexual couples: "To varying degrees, lesbian ex-lovers retain their ties to one another after their breakup and use these bonds to rebuild their lives. An ex-lover remains an important part of a woman's evolving identity: as a woman, as a lesbian, and as a participant in intimate relationships" (Becker 1988:211).

The other side of the "intimacy equals friendship" equation is the prospect that "friendship equals intimacy." Friendships between lesbians may be complicated by sexual attraction. This problem can be threatening to couples (heterosexual as well as lesbian, although the threat is likely to be more deeply submerged between heterosexual women). On the other hand, lesbians sometimes allow close friendships, with their unspoken potential, to balance their primary relationships. What is missing at home may be found elsewhere, and as long as the friendship does not become too threatening or turn into a sexual affair, it may help to sustain the primary relationship.

What is clear in these descriptions is that the crucial dimension is one of emotional closeness. Again and again, this theme prevails in discussions of lesbian couples. The desire for a close emotional connection seems to be the primary mark of lesbian relationships. Attachment, emotional involvement, intimacy, and general closeness are highly correlated with satisfaction in lesbian relationships. When their priorities for career or for relationship are compared, lesbian couples are more relationship-centered than heterosexual or gay male ones.[3] Although commitment to career is often high among lesbians, many find the conflict between choosing time for work and time for their partners difficult.

Again, this kind of data can be understood as relevant to the psychology of women as a whole, not just relevant to lesbian psychology. It reinforces the view that a need or desire for emotional intimacy, for feeling close, is characteristic of women's psychology. We would expect desire for closeness to be highly characteristic of relationships between women. Studies of women's adult development bear out this view, pointing to the role of close relationships and intimate friendships as part of the essential framework for women's continuing growth as adults (Hancock 1981; Berzoff 1989). If women's growth as adults rests upon intimacy and interrelatedness with others, relationships that afford greater intimacy hold special advantages. The high degree of intimacy in many lesbian relationships may nurture the continuing development of the individual women.

This dimension of lesbian relating may carry a particular unconscious valence, a somewhat intuitive recognition of its potential for developmental support. It may also mean that lesbian relationships are particularly vulnerable to impossible expectations, as both partners seek a special kind of fulfillment and weigh the relationship according to its ability to deliver it. This dimension of a relationship—its potential for supporting individual growth—is vital to every couple, unconsciously more often than consciously. It may be, however, that the focus on, or the concern with, closeness in lesbian relationships adds extra weight to the relationship's meaning.

The Press Toward Merger

Since many writers have identified merger or fusion as a major issue in clinical work with lesbian couples, the theme has tended to dominate the picture of lesbian psychology. Merger goes beyond mere closeness or attachment. It is a sense of *being* the other person rather than being like, connected to, or near the other. With merger the metaphorical boundary between self and other is changed or dissolved and a sense of union overtakes the sense of separateness.

At its most intense and pleasurable, falling in love is the quintessential experience of merger. Lovemaking is, in part, a pursuit of this psychic union. The loving gaze, the desire to touch, the sense of silent communion lovers share are means of creating and recreating the feeling of oneness in love. These heightened experiences of merger bring with them a sense of transformation, as one feels one's self to be utterly changed, renewed, or expanded by them. Psychoanalysts, at least until Kohut, tended to treat experiences of merger or fusion as pathological. A few psychoanalytic authors, however, have written about this transformative aspect of merger. For example, Ethel Person (1988) says:

> The fluidity of the ego enables the kind of interpenetration of selves that constitutes merger. . . . The exaltation of love is most of all attributable to the new expanded sense of self that results when two separate beings come together as one. In large measure, exaltation is made possible by the lovers' periodic achievement of "merger," with its sense of release from the burdens of the self, the immersion in something larger than self. (127–129)

Nathaniel Ross (1975) similarly compares falling in love to a mystical experience: both involve a sense of fusion or merger. Altering the boundary between self and other engenders regression to an undifferentiated state in which knowing and feeling are again united, enabling new experiences to be integrated.

Merger is not entirely defined by this exalted state however. A somewhat more mundane kind of merger exists (with less awareness) in a daily way for many couples. This is the merger of couples who have great difficulty feeling or being separate from each other, who think in terms of each other with every move, who feel guilty or anxious about interests, thoughts, and feelings that are *not* shared. Their individual selves have been given over to the fusion, and they may feel it is a necessity of the relationship not to retrieve them. Couples sometimes express this in terms of what their relationship permits them to experience.

JULIA AND ELAINE

Partners for four years, Julia, a twenty-seven-year-old black woman, and Elaine, a twenty-five-year-old white woman, expressed the limits of their relationship. Elaine said, "Julia makes me feel guilty when I go out with friends, so I can't do that." Julia said, "I think Elaine doesn't really like any of my friends, so I've had to give them up. I'm not sure now if I ever liked them myself."

In this example each woman experiences the other as controlling her feelings as well as behavior.

While many, if not all, intimate relationships, including friendships, probably involve experiences of merger, a prolonged or enduring fusion between partners can ultimately be destructive both to the individual sense of self and to the relationship. The couple founders in too much connectedness. One or both partners eventually feels the threat of loss of self and tries to emerge from their overly close union, but often this disrupts the relationship. The woman seeking to re-establish her sense of self may make desperate efforts to create a boundary between them, now by highlighting their differences instead of their similarities, by provoking fights, by sexually or emotionally withdrawing, by having an affair, or by leaving the relationship altogether. A balance of intimate connection and autonomy cannot be found within the relationship. This is the picture therapists often describe from clinical practice.

A decade ago much of the writing about lesbian couples, including my own, argued that merger is common to lesbian couples.[4] Social factors, intrapsychic ones, or a combination of both are used to explain this observation. For example, merger in lesbian couples may be a consequence of both homophobia and women's socialization. Women are expected to invest deeply in relationships; then, facing a hostile world, the lesbian couple tends to turn in on itself. This view also argues that the presence of children tends to dilute the intensity of a relationship, and that lesbian relationships are less likely to include children than heterosexual ones (another difference that is rapidly changing). Gay male couples face social hostility, as well, yet merger is not a primary issue in male couples. Indeed, the opposite is suggested: male needs for independence interfere with emotional closeness (Elise 1986).

Merger has also been described as a community phenomenon: a lesbian community serves as a haven for lesbians in an often unfriendly world. It sanctions the social differentness of lesbianism. Yet the community can demand a uniformity of values and identity that undercuts the individual need for differentiation. Susan Krieger questions: "What happens to female identity in an all-female society or, more broadly, what happens to the individual in a community of likeness?" (Krieger 1983:106).

Other women argue for a different perspective:

> Fusion in a couple context has little to do with lesbian identity; rather it is a heterosexist, male-defined concept. Fusion more accurately describes male-female relationships, in which part of the patriarchal plan is female subjugation to male identity. . . . The distinction between friends and lovers, for example, is heterosexually inspired and more descriptive of heterosexual than lesbian relationships. In the lesbian community, boundaries between romantic attachments and friendships are less well defined, affectionate bonding is common and valued, and the challenge of maintaining friendships with ex-lovers is supported. In addition to asking [as Krieger did], "What happens . . . to identity when so much that is consequential is hastened over and merged?" we might also ask, "What happens to identity when our bonds with other women weather the coming and goings of intimate involvement?" (Bristow and Pearn 1984:730)

This concern with applying concepts from heterosexual relationships directly to lesbian relationships is echoed by others who wish to understand lesbian relationships on their own terms by placing them in the center of the narrative. And, certainly, the nature of community within gay and lesbian culture has changed, from a superficial homogeneity to a sometimes factionalized emphasis on differences, corresponding to the prevalence of identity politics in the larger culture (Weston 1991).

A Boundary Dispute

The traditional psychoanalytic explanation of merger in lesbian couples is based on assumptions of pathology: homosexuality is an indication of "arrested development" or a lack of personal boundaries as a result of early childhood deficits. The intense fusion of the mother-child symbiotic bond has never been broken, and the individual cannot tolerate separateness. According to this perspective, as an adult the homosexual continues to require a re-creation of this interpersonal and intrapsychic bond (Socarides 1981; McDougall 1980).

There are two problems with this view. First, it fails to distinguish between merger and symbiosis. Merger is a common relational configuration, desired by most couples at some point in their relationship, as Person notes. Symbiosis is more primitive and more complete in its regressive pull than the kind of merger that adult relationships commonly engage in. In its ultimate fulfillment, symbiosis in adults equals psychosis, or utter loss of the reality of boundaries, identities, and the external world. (Couples may not always make this distinction, however, and fear of merger is sometimes founded upon distrust of one's own boundaries and fear that the line between merger and symbiosis is a fragile one.) These psychoanalysts tend to see merger as symbiosis and consequently see relationships between lesbians as deeply disturbed.

A symbiotic tie with the mother would make establishment of an identity so clearly differentiated from the mother's as a homosexual one unlikely in any case. Symbiotic bonds indicate an undifferentiated self, more likely to be expressed in lack of any sexual identity. The treatment of merger as inevitably pathological probably also derives from an assumption, common within psychoanalysis, that the relationship with the mother is always something to be grown away from rather than renewed in adult relationships.

Further evidence against this view is the evidence of gay male relationships. The pejorative psychoanalytic perspective considers all homosexuals, men as well as women, to be trapped in preoedipal symbiotic bonds. The relative lack of merger as a characteristic of male relationships undermines this view. The significant variable seems to be gender, not preoedipal pathology, a variable even more important than the social place of homosexual relations.

Some writers have understood merger through a psychodynamic approach to female development, in terms similar to Winnicott's paradoxical view of separation processes. Winnicott (1971) speaks of the baby's "separating-off of the not-me from the me" (11), which permits the mother to be seen as a person in her own right. Yet for Winnicott, separation, like independence, is not absolute. In play and in love, in the concept of potential space between self and other, one finds "the separation that is not a separation but a form of union" (98). Independence and separation are understood as relative states that fluctuate, always balancing dependence and connection.

Feminist writers in the 1970s addressed the question of gender differences in regard to psychological separateness. Nancy Chodorow's (1978) exploration of this question suggests that girls will experience more boundary confusion and greater difficulty with differentiation than boys because they share gender sameness with the mother. It is not only, or not even primarily, the daughter's awareness of this sameness, but the mother's that influences boundary development. A mother will likely experience her daughter as more like herself than she experiences her son to be. She will form a different relationship with her than with a son. As the child begins to be aware of gender and to develop an identity based on gender, differences will again be seen. A son will need to differentiate himself from mother more thoroughly in order to feel a sense of maleness, while a daughter does not require such clear differentiation to know herself female. She can continue in her sense of oneness with mother as she experiences herself to be female. For her, the boundary between self and other may remain more permeable.

In adult relationships these gender differences come to bear on the distinction between self and other between the partners. Women are more likely than men to seek a continuing sense of oneness in relationship (Jordan et al. 1991). With male partners, that search is less likely to be mirrored; in fact the male's clearer personal boundaries provide a relationship boundary both feel. The woman's boundaries are not pathologically absent, rather they are differently constructed. Her relational fluidity is both an asset and a liability, granting greater capacity for closeness and attunement on the one hand, but more difficulty with separateness and a sense of "not-me" on the other. Dorothy Dinnerstein (1976) believes that men's fear of "sinking back wholly into the helplessness of infancy" engenders a need for dominance and power and an intense fear of merger. Indeed, to some degree the legacy of infancy for all adults is fear of merger. This fear is perhaps what makes some theorists tend to pathologize merger.

Jean Baker Miller (1976) believes that "women's sense of self becomes very much organized around being able to make and then to maintain affiliation and relationships." She argues that a woman's self-esteem and sense of competence are based in emotional connections and that traditional theories are inadequate for understanding this aspect of women's psychology:

> The concept of a "self" as it has come down to us has encouraged a complex series of processes leading to a sense of separateness from others. . . . These realms delegated to women [tending to relatedness] . . . have not been incorporated into our perceptions as sources of growth, satisfaction and empowerment. (13–14)

Likewise, Janet Surrey envisions "the core self in women" unfolding through mutual empathic processes. A woman does not become "an isolated or separated autonomous individual" (Jordan et al. 1991:7).

Miller, Surrey, and other women from the Stone Center Institute at Wellesley College oppose Chodorow's and other object relations theorists' perspective to the extent that it retains an emphasis on achieving separateness as an essential developmental task. A woman's self is always a self-in-relation. They do not validate the liability perspective inherent in Chodorow's view of women's intrapsychic structuring. In their view women's embeddedness in interrelatedness is not problematic in any way; it simply signifies a difference between women's and men's development. Their viewpoint seems to idealize women's developmental path; at the same time, they have clearly made the crucial point that when women are looked at through the lens of male developmental theories, one sees pathology rather than difference.

Although the disagreements between feminist psychodynamic perspectives are significant ones, they commonly agree that women develop most fully within the matrix of their relatedness to others, not apart from it. Their sense of individuality must be found within this matrix, not outside of it, as may be the case for men. Other women's research establishes the significance of relatedness in women's development as adults as well. Carol Gilligan's (1982) study locates the sense of morality within relatedness to others, not in more abstract principles of right and wrong. Joan Berzoff's (1989) work demonstrates that friendships between women "catalyze their psychological development." Doris Silverman (1987) finds evidence of the special significance of attachment for girls even in infancy, suggesting that there may be a genetic predisposition in females toward bonding.

These writers indicate the centrality of attachment, relatedness, and interdependence as issues in women's development, the same issues that reverberate in lesbian relationships. This relational orientation in women's psychology is expressed, for example, in the tendency of lesbians to maintain ties to ex-lovers, a phenomenon not as common in heterosexual relationships. Both the value of attachment per se and the discomfort with separation are manifested here.

Although these views of women's development differ in certain ways, all point to the focal importance of relationships in women's lives. They argue that separation is never so clear-cut for women as it has been traditionally conceived and that both heterosexual and lesbian women experience a less-separate sense of self than men of either sexual orientation. Feminist psychoanalytic theory suggests that women's development continues within a context of great interrelat-edness—that indeed separation may be a defensive maneuver more required by males than females. These views echo the story of Demeter and Persephone, in which the turmoil and alternation of oneness and separateness forever continue. The phenomenon of merger in lesbian relationships is indicative of this difference between men and women, not between homosexuality vs. heterosexuality.

The Function of Merger

If a greater vulnerability to merger is a consequence of women's early development, it easily follows that merger would often be manifested in lesbian relationships. The gender sameness of lesbian couples invites an illusion of a more total sameness between the partners. And because both are women, the desire for oneness and fear of its regres-sive pull creates dynamic tension. Differences, real or projectively cre-ated, may be threatening, but they are also pursued. It is a complex experience, one that is not easily untangled.

CLAIRE AND ZOE

Claire and Zoe have been lovers for three years. Zoe, thirty-one, Jewish, from Manhattan, feels Claire is too passive and too dependent on her. She wants Claire to be more aggressive in the world, and more independent in their relationship, and criticizes Claire freely. Claire, thirty-eight, from a white, midwestern Catholic background, both agrees with and resists Zoe's opinion of her. She doesn't really want to be more aggressive, she likes closeness, and thinks she is independent enough in the relationship. She simply wants Zoe to stop being critical.

Zoe seems not to realize that Claire's assertion of her own values and her own way of being in the relationship is itself an independent act. She implicitly demands that Claire take on her own values yet somehow be independent of her. Claire appears to be the one maintaining the merger on a behavioral level—she even says that is exactly what she wants with Zoe—but her resistance to Zoe's demands says something else. Zoe seems more independent but is actually the one who cannot accept their differences. In demanding that they be alike, she demands the merger she also fears. Who is trying to maintain their oneness? Both, but in different ways. Their struggle with merger is layered with paradox and creates a relational structure that functions with some stability.

This formulation has other implications as well. It suggests that a relationship between two women characterized by merger is not inherently a troubled one. The greater fluidity of women's ego boundaries is both a liability and an asset (as men's more rigid boundaries are). It allows greater intimacy, but requires more psychological work to establish or maintain a sense of self not entirely at the whims of relationship. As a corollary to this view, one can understand that a relationship that participates in degrees of merger may provide a favorable arena for a woman's continuing development, a view I will explore later. We may wonder then whether heterosexual women do not sometimes feel frustrated in their desire for merger with their male partners.

The picture that emerges out of clinical work with lesbian couples is by nature skewed toward problematic experiences. The negative consequence of continued merger in a relationship is the difficulty of knowing who one is apart from the other. The costs of this kind of merger can be high for the women involved: losing their sense of autonomy or their sexual expressiveness, being in perpetual conflict (in an effort to differentiate), or even needing to end the relationship. A flexible merger in a lesbian relationship nevertheless has positive aspects. The continuing tension between merger and separateness as each partner contends with fear of merger and desire for merger extends the process of differentiation. This struggle may contribute to a woman's developmental journey. Eventually, optimally, a woman may become aware of both sides of the polarity (desire to merge and desire to separate) within herself.

A common pattern that lesbian couples present in therapy is one in which one partner pursues closeness, the other pursues boundaries, not unlike Claire and Zoe. Each is unable to move out of her position. Via projective identification, each has disowned an aspect of her own needs—either for closeness or distance—and projected it onto her lover, who identifies with the projection and carries it for both of them. Each perceives her partner as having an unchanging need, for closeness or distance, which she must resist in order to satisfy her own opposite need. This perception does not describe either woman accurately, but it shifts the locus of tension from the inner world, where it may feel too uncomfortable, to the outer world, where it is a different kind of problem to be managed.

This kind of enduring projective identification requires interpersonal maneuvering to induce the one to experience the disavowed feelings of the other. As one partner becomes more distant, her distancing provokes the other to pursue. Now their roles are established in the relationship, and they may carry out this polarization for very long periods of time, sometimes for the entire relationship. Each partner expresses her own need for closeness or distance and her partner's need for it as well. The partner no longer experiences this need as her own. Her own self-knowledge and development are limited by this fusion.

Although complementary relationships are established through projective identification, this enduring state of merger is a defensive use of projective identification in which part of one's self is thoroughly disowned and one's self feels depleted. When partners are unable to process each other's projections, they begin to act them out in ways destructive to the relationship. Rather than the drawing together of opposites to fulfill their complementary potential, there is antagonism. Polarizing tends to render differences more extreme; they may eventually become so extreme that a repelling force is generated. Then the need for separateness is expressed through action—often destructively for the relationship—such as withdrawal, purposeless fighting, having affairs, etc. The relationship may end for lack of any better alternative.

On the other hand, if the two partners tolerate such polarizing and eventually begin to reinternalize the lost parts of the self, something transformative may occur in the process. (This is where therapy is of help. In fact, the transformational power of therapy often relies upon the same process.) The need, internalized again, for intimacy or autonomy may be less threatening to a woman after she has encountered her partner's experience with it. Each now finds herself in the psychic realm necessary for her own growth, struggling with the internal tension between autonomy and relatedness. As Polly Crisp (1988) has suggested, the capacity for receiving and containing projective identifications may indicate some underlying vulnerability or it may be evidence of a mature sensibility. I would add that these two possibilities are not necessarily contradictory. In this ambivalent merger pattern we see a reflection of the need for differentiation within connectedness that is an essential aspect of female development.

Some writers argue that merger within relationship inevitably fosters growth and self-affirmation, that it is clearly an asset. A relatively flexible merger allows partners to mirror each other and to idealize each other in just the ways that foster growth and well-being (Mitchell 1988; Mencher 1990). They assert that a particularly beneficial kind of complementarity is generated here.

Arguments that merger is the pattern of intimacy desired by women in general and is one of the benefits of lesbian relationships, unfortunately, do not always distinguish between intimacy and merger or between degrees of merger. They emphasize the "mutual engagement, mutual empathy, and mutual empowerment" of merger (Mencher 1990), but these qualities are not peculiar to merger; they are expressive of intimacy itself. The dynamics of merger that others have described can generate anxiety rather than satisfaction in a relationship.

Some empirical support does exist for the notion that merging between women enhances development. Joan Berzoff (1989) studied friendships between heterosexual women, women who had such close relationships with other women that they were valued as much or more than their work, children, husbands, and health. (These women seem to reflect a kind of bisexual heterosexuality—at least in

an emotional sense. Their relationships sound like contemporary editions of "passionate friendships.") The women who had had the most
intense experiences of merger or threatened loss of identity in their
relationships with their best friends were also the women who scored
highest on measurements of ego development, indicating highly
developed autonomous functioning.

These findings throw into question the assumption that merging is
antithetical to autonomy or mature development. Berzoff notes:

> Empathy and access to the deepest inner experiences of others
> requires a high level of self differentiation. Traditional theories
> which have held that finding oneself means moving away from
> others do not fully account for adult women's experiences of
> empathy and connectedness. . . . Such temporary losses of self
> need to be understood not as regressive or pathological losses,
> but as potential articulations of the self in the context of an inti-
> mate other. (1989:105–106)

These different views of the function and value of merger suggest
that the concept itself needs further delineation. Merger can be conceived as having at least two dimensions: intensity and fluidity. An
intense, rigidly maintained fusion is at the extremes of both dimensions and may indicate an incapacity for separateness, while a more
fluid but nevertheless deep merger may be inherent in any passionate
intimacy. A fixed but less intense merger signifies a relational stalemate
that may eventually tolerate some degree of autonomy. Weak and
highly fluid experiences of merger probably occur with great frequency in encounters with friends, lovers, and partners in all kinds of
endeavors. In between are many variations, with relative benefits and
relative psychological risks.

Some relationships between women fall immediately and happily
into a state of merger that endures for years, often quite well. When the
relationship hits its own midlife crisis, it is likely to become intolerant
of their fusion, then requiring of them the arduous work of reestab-
lishing their bond on a new foundation. The evolution of the relationship is of course entwined with each woman's individual develop-

ment. Other couples are drawn immediately into a merger, but one or both women may find this highly threatening, and the relationship establishes itself on a basis of stable or unstable struggle: they may endure this way, they may evolve gradually to a more comfortably separate state, or they may break up. Many couples who begin their relationship on a more differentiated basis eventually wear down their differences and develop a contented merger that tolerates enough degrees of freedom for each to continue on her own path, a compatible and agreeable drifting in and out of fusion.

In her work on the conception and creation of lesbian and gay families and kinship bonds, Kath Weston challenges the notion of merger altogether. She writes, "as metaphor, merging depends upon culturally specific constructions of an essentialized self that can be lost and alienated as well as discovered and loved" (1991:153). Western culture, and especially psychoanalytic culture, has indeed relied upon the idea of an essentialized self (Winnicott's "true self" is one very good example of this notion). Much of psychodynamic therapy revolves around furthering the development of this sense of self, and many individuals, inside and outside of therapy, tend to conceptualize themselves likewise. This socially constructed self is at risk of stalemate via merger, while in other cultures what we identify as merger might be normative.

The currency of merger as a concept within lesbian culture has created both the sense and fear of merger between women. Lesbian couples, as Marny Hall (1995) notes, now come to therapy already self-diagnosed. She writes, "when . . . my clients came in caricaturing themselves as "textbook lesbians" and "merger queens," I laughed ruefully and wondered whether my colleagues and I . . . were authoring a new genre of lesbian self-doubt" (17). These critiques do not invalidate merger as a concept but relativize it, placing it within the bounds of a socially influenced psychology—as of course all psychology is—and again reiterating the problem with the concept of pathology itself.

As a culturally constructed, even a culturally induced, state, merger seems to be experienced at a deep level individually, deep enough to be amenable to psychodynamic analysis as long as that analysis remains grounded in the interpersonal rather than the strictly intrapsychic, realm. Within a strictly intrapsychic realm it is susceptible to interpretations of primitive pathology; interpersonally, it is understood to be created out of a complicated interaction between individual psychology, perhaps certain rather inevitable dynamics of intimacy between humans, and a mutual intermingling of cultural influences, all of which might be interpreted otherwise in a different setting.

Lesbian relationships are generally more relationship-centered than those of other couples. A recurring theme is the salience of both sameness and difference, the tension between emotional closeness and distance, and the potential of lesbian relationships to support individual development. It may be that women's psychological development imparts a special vulnerability to merger, something both problematic and potentially transformative. The recurrence of this theme indicates the desire for a partner who will match one's interests and needs but somehow also be an other, the optimal relational ground for growth. Person's study of love relationships repeatedly points to the healing and transformative potential of love, intimacy, and merger: "Love does more than restore; love catalyzes change in the self. Love may be regressive, but it is also progressive, giving direction and content to the maturation of the self" (1988:93). Here a kind of progressive merger, capable of catalyzing change, is conceptualized.

6

Themes in Lesbian Relationships:
The Balance of Power

A relationship between two adults that is both loving and sexual has more elements of mystery than rationality to it. Part of the power of erotic relationships lies in their ability to unconsciously recreate the lost experience of sensuality and safety that each adult once knew, even if only briefly or sporadically, as an infant in the arms of her or his mother. This experience, which is lost to conscious recall, is remembered by the body and evoked in intimate adult contact. In heterosexual relationships the evocation is more direct and complete for a man than for a woman, as he once again loses himself in loving physical contact with a woman. As Dorothy Dinnerstein says, "Since the first parent is female, heteroerotic feeling has deeper roots in infancy for men than for women" (1976:66). A woman is one step removed from the intensity: "In the sexual recapitulation of the infant-mother interplay, [the woman] has more of a sense than [the man] does of embodying the powerful mother within herself: a greater part of her than of his reliving of the infant role is vicarious, through the other person" (67).

Only in lesbian relationships do women once again experience this reconnection directly. For many women involvement with another woman is like reclaiming a lost history, an opportunity full of joy and promising more fulfilling intimacy. Intimacy becomes a struggle, however, when the threats, disappointments, and injuries of childhood are also reactivated. This triggering of early experience always occurs in adult love affairs, consciously or unconsciously. Because they include such intimate bodily contact, they evoke one's buried primal history.

The child's early experience with parents creates some kind of template for future emotional as well as physical involvements. Because women provide most of the early parenting, the mother-child relationship tends to be a more significant determinant. Between heterosexual women intimate relationships—close emotional if not physical ties—also evoke traces of the early mother-daughter relationship. In this chapter I discuss difficulties in lesbian relationships that may also be found between women friends. Chapter 4 explored women's sense of vulnerability with other women based on emotional/erotic rejection by the mother. The struggles described in this chapter suggest another level of vulnerability women sometimes feel in relation to each other.

All relationships must in some way negotiate three major issues: the balance of power, the pull toward and away from dependency, and the roles involved in nurturing. In heterosexual intimacy these roles tend to be assigned according to gender. Between women they are negotiated interpersonally and often rather subtly. These issues hold the potential for mutuality and equality, but they may also be intensely charged with meaning and struggle, and intimacy can be difficult.

The Balance of Power

Empirical studies find that lesbians greatly value equality in their relationships. The degree to which they feel the relationship is a good one is often a direct consequence of whether it is judged to be an equal one. Lesbian relationships also seem to achieve in actuality a more nearly equal balance of power than all other kinds of relationships.[1] Decisions about how a couple will live together, spend money, play, and socialize are generally founded in mutuality, without the division of labor according to social gender roles. Heterosexual couples, in spite of their best efforts, often fall back into stereotypical roles around the house, while lesbians seem to divide up the chores by personal preference, leaving both traditionally male and female tasks to each partner.[2]

Empirical measures of equality and decision making suggest concern not only with these concrete manifestations of power in a relationship but with more elusive dimensions as well. Emotional dependence takes on greater significance as a variable of power. One gives and receives power in dependency and interdependency. The level of emotional involvement and commitment to the relationship determines one's subjective sense of power. The more committed partner may feel she has relatively less power in relation to her less involved lover. Finding a perfect balance does not seem to be easy, even in the absence of socially designated roles, and lesbian couples who seek therapy are often struggling with some perceived imbalance of power. One might ask why lesbians in particular hold this value so high and put such effort into its fulfillment. I think the answer requires both social and psychodynamic explanations.

Many lesbians are feminists, and, for some, their feminism preceded their lesbianism. Lesbian relationships hold a special appeal for these women because they represent freedom from male dominance and the inequality of heterosexual relationships. Many lesbians recall having an early awareness of the requirements placed on women in heterosexual culture. Their movement toward lesbianism has been at least in part a movement away from the limitations of gender roles. Lesbians are not simply relieved of these burdens however. By virtue of their homosexuality, lesbian women lose social and political standing: they lack access to male power and they are members of a devalued minority group. Social and political equality are thus highly valued but painfully confounded. This struggle comes home in personal relationships, where equality is difficult to maintain.

Deeper roots of this concern lie in the legacy of the mother-child relationship. The fundamental inequality of the parent-child relationship is a kind of narcissistic wound even in the most favorable developmental picture. Each developmental advance grants children more ability to assert themselves, and they eagerly try to establish new ranking in relation to mother. Boys grow up to do this quite thoroughly:

they may have relationships with women in which they are clearly dominant. For girls, there is no such ready escape. Heterosexual women sometimes find vicarious reparation for this wound by identifying with male partners. They tolerate male dominance in unconscious collusion with the wish to subdue the mother. As Dorothy Dinnerstein says, "*The crucial psychological fact is that all of us, female as well as male, fear the will of woman*" (1976:161). In every relationship with a woman, there is the shadow of the mother.

For lesbians, then, it is not simply, nor even primarily, the power of men that threatens inequality but the balance of power between the two women, the threatening power of woman/mother. Women struggle to free themselves from the will of the mother in their resistance to their partner's will. The distinction between actual inequalities and felt experiences of powerlessness may be confused by this threat, so that seemingly minor differences carry unconscious significance. The female matrix of development, the mother-daughter bond itself, gives these issues emotional charge and makes them threatening to both. Lesbian relationships involve two individuals dealing in the same arena here. Each partner brings her own experience from this matrix up against another woman. In unconscious terms, the lover is guilty by association.

Jessica Benjamin's (1988) analysis of gender relations suggests another dimension to issues of power and dominance. Imbalance in the parents' roles, mother's lack of subjectivity within the family, and the difficulty for daughters in identifying with fathers leaves women with a weak sense of self. Her development slants her desires toward a strong partner who will dominate. Dinnerstein poses a mother who is frightening in her strength and power; Benjamin poses a mother who is disturbing in her weakness. This apparent contradiction is resolved by understanding that Dinnerstein speaks primarily of the mother of infancy and focuses on the mother's power within her relationship with her child. Benjamin gives the father more importance than Dinnerstein does and focuses on the mother's position within the family structure. Thus the mother who is so powerful with the young child is also the less powerful mother vis-à-vis the father and the larger world. Their views are complementary and both underscore not only the significance of the mother in the child's psyche but also the psychological cost of unbalanced roles in heterosexual families.

If Benjamin's description of heterosexual relations and women's submissiveness within them is accurate, lesbians are not necessarily exempt. They may also unconsciously desire strong partners as well as find them threatening. This paradox suggests the potential for a complex, conflicted concern between women for where power lies. The partner represents both the feared mother and the devalued mother. Her own self representations embody both as well.

Conflict is important in any relationship. Out of the initial period of attachment and intense intimacy, a couple usually emerges into a period of territorial struggle. Individual boundaries are reestablished here, and the strength of the relationship is under scrutiny. Conflict is threatening to many women, however, for it appears to signal impending rupture or separation. When the high value placed on intimacy in lesbian relationships is accompanied by an equally high value on autonomy, these needs can seem to interfere with each other. The difficulty of satisfying both may lead to a long-term process of negotiation and renegotiation. Recalling the last chapter, autonomy and differentiation are recurring developmental tasks for many women, psychological ground that must be crossed again and again. The concern with equality is a concern with individuality as well as power. The ideals that are valued most in lesbian relationships put great demands on each woman's personal development. Inability to satisfy these impossible desires can be interpreted as a failure of the relationship.

Negotiating the Power

In therapy many lesbians express a determination not to be in a less powerful position in a relationship. With some individuals or couples the issue is out in the open: one partner feels her lover holds more power in the relationship and wants this imbalance to change. In other cases one or both partners defend well against feelings of powerlessness, and the issue is covert. Locked in a subtle ongoing battle, each defends against feeling the other's power. What is often more apparent than the struggle itself is its effects: their capacity for intimacy is diminished.

Any number of differences are singled out by the couple as a source of inequality or imbalance of power. (Differences are also sometimes resisted per se, of course, because they obstruct the wish for merger.) Unequal division of labor, money, or recognition, inequality in emotional vulnerability and felt dependency, differences in race, ethnic background, class, etc., can be difficult to cope with, as well as differences in personal qualities or assets such as self-confidence, verbal or physical abilities, or talents. Some couples handle differences or inequalities between them without great difficulty. Others are preoccupied with them. Actual inequalities and felt experiences of powerlessness are not always distinguished.

Two clinical examples of lesbian relationships embroiled in power struggles illustrate the problems:

KATHRYN AND MAIA

Kathryn, thirty, white, raised in southern California, and Maia, thirty-four, Asian-American, raised in northern California, came to therapy because, according to Maia, they fought too much. Kathryn complained that Maia was so independent that Kathryn couldn't get really close to her. Maia was more self-assured, while Kathryn often exposed her insecurity and vulnerability. Maia got her way most of the time. Kathryn had become defensive and resistant to intimacy with Maia. She handled her perception of Maia's greater power by controlling the frequency of their contact and by starting fights. She thought she probably ought to leave the relationship.

JACKIE AND PAM

Jackie and Pam, two white women raised in West Coast suburbia, had been together two years, but their relationship was on the verge of dissolving when they came to therapy. At thirty-six Jackie was well-educated, highly successful at work, owned their house, and wanted to be settled down. Pam at twenty-five was unsettled, had left college after her second year, and had not found work that suited her. She wanted to be a writer but had lost sight of her goal and now had a low-paying job in a bookstore. Recently she'd had an affair with another woman. In therapy she began to articulate that she felt over-powered by Jackie and wasn't sure who she was any more.

With Kathryn and Maia the power struggle revolved around psychological and emotional differences. Kathryn felt their differences to be unbearable and was tormented by a sense of powerlessness. I'll return to their case later. With Jackie and Pam, there were many concrete differences such as age, income, education, and success. Pam's experience of powerlessness might have been less disturbing with a man; it might have been perceived as natural, since these differences are ones that many heterosexual relationships rest on. Perhaps, as Dinnerstein says, such inequalities feel safer with a man than with another woman. The outcome of therapy for Jackie and Pam was a decision to break up. Pam felt she would never be able to hold her own with Jackie, and Jackie began to question whether she was protecting herself from her own insecurity, fear of rejection, or fear of being less powerful in a relationship. The inequality between them was striking, yet, again, in a heterosexual relationship, it may have been little noticed; the potentially positive aspects of their breakup might have been missed in therapy.

Who's the Mom? Dependency Issues

Issues with dependency can take a different turn in lesbian relationships. The familiar struggle of women against overdependence on others may be primary for women in traditional roles, and lesbians can also be caught in a cycle of dependency on others, but the opposite can be just as true—dependency can be irrationally feared. Dependency may be feared because it represents identification with the old

sense of heterosexual femininity she has rejected as destructive to
women's, her own, integrity. However, she may also be irrationally
repelled by things too "feminine," such as passivity, vulnerability, or
dependence, reflecting an unconscious fear of womanness, an internalization of women's devaluation.

A woman who fears or even hates her own womanness will pro-
ject this onto her lover and feel further devalued herself by dependency on her. She will probably maintain a safe distance from her and
these feelings. Her own needs for dependency will be denied, and
she'll be psychologically isolated, even within a relationship. In the
case of Kathryn and Maia above, Maia is afraid of dependency on
another woman. She controls the fear by controlling her vulnerability. The case of Alicia presents a different example.

ALICIA

Alicia, a thirty-six-year-old white Protestant-bred woman from the
southwest, has a history of short-term relationships, each less than a
year and a half. Typically, she falls in love quite intensely, then after a few
months becomes disillusioned by her lover and begins to pull away.
When her lover tries to hold on or protests her distancing, Alicia is
annoyed that her freedom is being questioned. She gets angry and soon
leaves the relationship. Alicia lives very well on her own, earning a
good income. She travels by herself on vacations and is quite capable
of entertaining herself, yet she wishes she could have a relationship that
lasted longer. She came to therapy confused, asking whether relationships are really possible. Why do other women always want to possess
her? She is depressed and wonders if she should just reconcile herself
to being alone. Terrified of her own unrecognized dependency needs
and appalled by other women's, as soon as Alicia begins to feel dependent, she backs off, not understanding her fears but controlled by them.

When one woman is more dependent than the other in a relationship, both are usually conflicted about it. Consciously the more self-

sufficient woman is proud of her autonomy, and both of them may disparage the other's lack of it, i.e., her traditionally feminine position. However, internalization of gender-typed values is so powerful that unconsciously the self-sufficient one may also fear that she is in fact masculine—and the dependent one may feel unconsciously reassured in her more traditionally feminine role.

Another frequent source of conflict in lesbian relationships is, Who takes care of whom? Women are expected to be nurturers. In a lesbian relationship that expectation can be revised: at last one doesn't have to be the caretaker and may actually be nurtured instead. Jennifer and Natalie present an example of conflict over nurturing attention.

JENNIFER AND NATALIE

Jennifer and Natalie, both thirty-nine and Jewish, both from middle-class East Coast families, had been together for eighteen months. Jennifer was angry and disillusioned because whenever she was upset and turned to Natalie, Natalie backed off. Natalie thought Jennifer was upset too often and expected too much from her. She also felt that whenever she was angry or unhappy and expressed it to Jennifer, Jennifer got angry or hurt in response and the focus shifted to *her* feelings. Both of them felt wounded and frustrated. Both felt less than hopeful that the other could meet her needs, even though initially each felt the other to be someone who understood and responded to her more fully than anyone else ever had.

Conflict over nurturing manifests itself many ways: a refusal to nurture, a refusal to be nurtured, a demand for constant attention, an insistence on giving more than is wanted, a sense of betrayal at having to ask or specify what one wants. These problems can express conflicts over autonomy vs. dependence and may reflect early narcissistic wounds. However, this issue is related specifically to gender also.

Most women experience some measure of guilt or anxiety about how they do or don't take care of others. Many find it easier to give than to receive; their self-esteem is inextricably tied to giving. At the same time, resentment or anger may be hidden behind the giving, especially when their own needs are being neglected. Giving may also be a covert attempt to draw attention to one's own needs. A relationship between two women will inevitably stir such conflicts, if for no other reason than simply because women are so deeply associated with nurturing. Whatever the old wounds are, they are likely to be reopened.

Gender-Based Psychodynamics

Adding a gender-based perspective to traditionally understood psychodynamics adds missing pieces to an understanding of lesbian relationships. The convergence of psychodynamics and sociodynamics, as elucidated by many feminist analytic writers, creates problems for women in autonomy and sense of self. The situation is not simply negative; women's greater capacity for empathy, deep relatedness, and perhaps intuition are also part of this legacy.

The process of separation–individuation is never so complete, for men or women, as to preclude fear of reengulfment in the original mother–child unity and subsequent loss of self. Margaret Mahler describes this fear as "the defense against the perpetual longing of the human being for reunion with the erstwhile symbiotic mother, a longing that threatens individual entity and identity and therefore, has to be warded off even beyond childhood" (Mahler, Pine, and Bergman 1975:290). Physical intimacy arouses unconscious wishes to recapture that lost union. For both heterosexual men and lesbians, relationships evoke this longing (and defenses against it) probably more strongly than for gay men and heterosexual women, because their relationships involve intimacy with a woman's body. (Again, the distinction between symbiosis and merger is important here. Mahler writes of the symbiotic threat as a universal but impossible longing, impossible because it represents a complete loss of self, an undoing of personal boundaries so complete that psychosis prevails and reality is lost. Merger is a fantasy of loss of self, one that can be safely indulged when personal boundaries exist to a sufficient degree to retrieve the self.)

As noted earlier, male defenses against engulfment in the mother are established early, as part of their developing gender identity. Chodorow argues that emphasis on differentness and separateness are essential defenses of male identity:

> Maleness is more conflictual and problematic [than femaleness]. Underlying, or built into core male gender identity is an early, nonverbal, unconscious, almost somatic sense of primary one-ness with the mother, an underlying sense of femaleness that continually ... challenges and undermines the sense of maleness ... [Men] come to emphasize differences, especially in situations that evoke anxiety. ... Separateness and difference as a compo-nent of differentiation become more salient. (1978:13)

Because mothers relate to sons as Other more than daughters, they give boys further experience with a sense of difference. Boys develop a firmer, albeit partly defensive, sense of a separate self, and the bound-ary around the self is less fluid or more rigid. For a woman there is a less defensive boundary, and in lesbian relationships boundaries are doubly permeable, more fluid on both sides. The threat of loss of self may feel greater. While this may appear simply to be a return to the issue of merger, I am distinguishing these issues to introduce other elements of the struggle (although at times the distinction will be arti-ficial). Out of these struggles against early dependency and loss of self, conflicts over power, adult dependency, and nurturance emerge.

Differences do not carry the same rewarding function of establish-ing the girl's gender identity that they do for boys. They signal some-thing to be lost with no compensating sense of gain. This lack of ease with differences means that the other, the different one, is felt to be powerful, while one's own self is felt to be small, weak, and perhaps unloved. To return to Kathryn and Maia, Kathryn constantly experi-enced a sense of being less powerful than Maia. Maia's defenses allowed her to appear somewhat invulnerable, but the actual differ-ences between them were not so real. Kathryn chafed under fears of losing herself with Maia, of allowing herself to be dominated; in fact, she could be quite assertive and hold her own ground. Her feeling of

powerlessness in relation to Maia was exaggerated. Exploring her fantasies about Maia's power helped her to grasp both the reality and the
unreality of her fears and to contain them enough to remain in the
relationship rather than flee. As she explored them, she recognized that
in a previous relationship she had felt herself to be the stronger one
and was equally uncomfortable with that position.

How are power struggles to be resolved in a lesbian relationship?
Exploring the parameters may give some perspective: how real is the
inequality of power and on what is it based? Do the women experience each other as adversaries and do they actually undermine each
other? (Who ultimately is the intrapsychic adversary?) Are their struggles valuable and constructive or otherwise? Power struggles can help
individuals define themselves more fully or they can be perpetual,
obsessive, and futile. The question each woman must grapple with is,
Do I need to hold on in the struggle or do I need to get over it? Some
battles have an imperative quality, signaling that they serve another
psychological function. Other fights are clearly defining territory and
establishing mutual autonomy. Two women who are each willful, self-
determined, and independent, for example, will likely have to go
through some battles with each other.

A woman's growth into autonomy is often a longer process than a
man's. Much of this process has occurred in the context of her relationship with her mother, positively or negatively. Being with another
woman will no doubt recall the earlier struggle and recreate unresolved parts of it. The relationship may be an impetus to further individuation by highlighting those unresolved issues.

Dependency is intertwined with issues of power: the compulsion
to avoid dependency arises from defenses against that early dependency on a woman. Again, the unconscious association of the lover
and the mother in their femaleness intensifies this struggle. There is
another factor as well: a sufficient period of genuine, developmentally
necessary, secure dependence as a child seems to be less likely for girls
than for boys. Jane Flax (1978) and Paula Caplan (1981) have both
noted that girls are not allowed the same real dependence when
infants and toddlers that boys are. The mother's own conflicts about

being female are easily projected onto a daughter. Caplan cites research that

> mothers are tolerant of baby boys' rituals and requirements at mealtime but insist on quick and unfussy eating by girls. . . . Girls are usually weaned earlier than boys, a practice that seems to be related to a greater comfort in keeping boys dependent on mothers. . . . They are requiring more self-control, more adult and less troublesome behavior on the part of their daughters. (28)

Flax states that girls are given less adequate emotional nurturance during separation-individuation. Both Flax and Caplan argue that physical nurturance of daughters is especially conflicted. For the heterosexual mother physical contact is not only potentially laden with forbidden incestuous feelings, as it is with sons, but touches on homophobic feelings as well. Chapter 4 explored this difficulty more fully; here I would simply note that the daughter's early years of dependency are hampered by such maternal conflicts, leaving her feeling deprived and in conflict about dependency, especially on women.

As they grow older, daughters begin to perceive the devaluation of women; they may come to see a mother who is less powerful in the family and in the culture (and even in the mother's own self-image). Initially the daughter longs to be like her powerful mother; later she learns to dissociate herself from her. She would prefer anything to identifying with her mother—but then she really has no choice. She is a woman, like her. The ambivalence of this identification makes for an uneasy peace in a lesbian relationship, especially when the contradictions are projected onto her partner. It can also create a similar vulnerability in friendships between women.

A relationship with another woman also arouses unconscious wishes to relive dependency in a more gratifying way. By avoiding dependency on another woman, some women fend off this conflicted wish. Women like Maia or Alicia who avoid dependency feelings may be just as needy behind their defenses as the partners they disparage. Intimacy with another woman threatens these defenses, leaving them with the possibility of feeling very vulnerable to early feelings of loss, woundedness, fear, and rage.

Ambivalence about nurturance is closely related to dependency issues. To be fed, held, and tended physically and emotionally is the child's first need. It is the first battleground, too, and again girls seem to suffer deprivation here more than boys. The same conflicts about being female that affect early-stage dependency in mother-daughter relationships determine how a woman will nurture her daughter. Caplan's report that mothers have less tolerance of daughters' idiosyncratic eating habits is only one example. Women's conflicts about nurturance and identification as women show most glaringly in the preoccupation with thinness and restrained eating that many adolescent and adult women have. Obsession with food, on the one hand, and with trying to be thin, on the other, reflect an impossible, contradictory attempt to nurture oneself while denying the body. The devaluation of women and the fact that women do essentially all the early parenting become deeply entangled here.

When girls are raised to forego their own needs and take care of others, they are usually taught this by their mothers—who have had the same experience as daughters. Often the daughter is asked to meet her mother's needs rather than her own, a request more acceptable to the mother with her daughters than with her sons. Caplan describes this process:

> Society gives the mothers the task of teaching daughters to be nurturant and self-sacrificing, as they themselves are supposed to be. It is a natural outgrowth of this situation that, as part of her training in responding to the needs of others, the daughter of a lonely and insecure mother will be taught to meet the mother's needs as well. Insofar as the daughter tries to meet those needs, to that extent will her own needs for nurturance go unmet. Thus the daughter grows up feeling inadequately nurtured. When she becomes a mother, she will have unmet needs and may turn to her own daughter, hoping the daughter will meet them. (1981:17)

Or the grown daughter may turn to her lover, if her lover is a woman. It is not surprising, then, that a woman may respond with fear or anger to another woman's expectation that she take care of her. A woman who doesn't want to nurture or is unable to let herself be nurtured may be fending off an overwhelming wish to be taken care of as well as deep resentment about her deprivation. As the nurturing child to her mother, she now fears any woman's needs and is alienated from her own.

For Jennifer and Natalie, the two women who felt unnurtured by each other, their issues were intertwined. Therapy required singling out a number of different threads for each of them. Jennifer's mother's own wounded narcissism required Jennifer to intuit and tend her needs, and the mother could not nurture Jennifer with much empathy. Now Jennifer experienced shame over her neediness and her acute sensitivity. She believed that her lover, then her therapist, could intuit the wounds, so any failure of perception was probably intended. After her rage and mistrust came out and, gradually, after much empathy, an awareness that Natalie did not intend to humiliate her when she needed some attention began to take hold. Her anger over Natalie's own expectations of emotional attention diminished; she began to tolerate Natalie saying no. In effect, she began to make a distinction at an unconscious level between Natalie and her mother.

Natalie, on the other hand, had consciously determined not to be trapped into a nurturing role in her adult relationships. Her mother relied on her for emotional contact and support, especially after her own mother died when Natalie was six. In the beginning of her relationship with Jennifer, Natalie used her early training as caretaker to stay closely attuned to Jennifer. She resented this, however, and soon rebelled by withdrawing, leaving Jennifer feeling betrayed. Natalie was convinced that if she lowered her guard, she would be propelled back into the nurturing role that was endless. She became rigid and self-righteous as she defended against Jennifer's need. On the other hand, she could not express her own well. Therapy involved many months of going back and forth through these blocks, affirming her fear and the anger related to past deprivations and facing the reality that adult relationships do not make up for early losses.

All of these issues are variations on the theme of old fears versus strong attraction. The fears lie dormant until a woman becomes involved with another woman. The intimacy of lesbian relationships, perhaps more than any other kind of relationship, approaches the intensity of the mother–daughter relationship. Fear of reengulfment in the mother–daughter history can be a strong unconscious barrier between women. Individually varied early experiences as a daughter come to bear forcefully on these more universal issues. The issues are usually intertwined; conflicts over power, nurturing, and dependence link up with each other to create patterns that may be difficult to comprehend.

Traditionally, psychology has presumed lesbian relationships to be pathological per se. Conflicts like the ones I am describing have shown up in clinical cases, and a presumption was often made that the women were lesbian precisely because they had such conflicts. Women raised in patriarchal culture, where gender inequities are the established basis of family life, inevitably have trouble with both a sense of self and a sense of separateness. It seems unlikely that women would not encounter some of these conflicts in a relationship with another woman. If a woman's capacity for intensity and intimacy is heightened in a relationship with another woman, who shares a similar capacity, their intimacy invites these kinds of problems as well.

Inevitably, lesbian relationships require women to grapple with issues related to mother, and we might also say that they afford women an incomparable opportunity to do so. The maturing of a relationship between two women as lovers or as friends often signifies the resolution of implicit negotiations between them. These negotiations may involve explicit issues important in their own right, but their apparent meaning easily conceals another. Resolution rests on each woman making peace with her own internalized mother—identifying with or differentiating from her to a greater degree, participating in her power and redeeming her devaluation as best she can—and perhaps seeing her actual mother more realistically, sometimes even understanding and forgiving her. It also involves making peace somehow with her partner's internalized mother, as she is projected onto her. Lesbians often acknowledge the degree to which their mothers seem to be present in their adult relationships and resist the intrusion, as if it can be prevented. Sometimes making peace means accepting this legacy and allowing it to evolve into something satisfying.

7 | Lesbian Sexuality/Female Sexuality: Searching for Sexual Subjectivity

Sociobiology posits inherent differences between men and women's sexuality, based on its reproductive significance. According to ethologists, the female is preoccupied with the fitness of her sexual partner for fathering healthy children, supporting her, and protecting her during her mothering years, ensuring the continuation of her own genetic heritage; the male is concerned with impregnating as many females as possible, increasing his chances of a genetic future (Batten 1992). In humans the same instinctual desires are presumed to operate, just slightly out of awareness. They are manifested in the stereotypical woman's attraction to an older, richer, and more powerful man and the stereotypical man's interest in younger women (whose fertility is high) and in nonmonogamy. Psychodynamic theory obviously posits other bases (intrapsychic and interpersonal family dynamics) for sexual patterns and partner choices.

Sociobiology acknowledges the role of cultural representations—their power to shape internal life and external behavior—but its view is that biology will often override culture or at least strongly influence the individual. Psychoanalytic theory has not contributed much analysis of the role of social imagery in shaping individual desire. The question is, Do cultural images of sexual desire follow from innate interests or do they construct them? The diversity of sexual expression across cultures and historical time challenges the adequacy of a biologically based view of human sexuality. Psychodynamic theory, keeping its focus narrowly within the individual and the family, also fails to account for such cross-cultural and historical diversity. Western cultural norms are treated as universals requiring little elaboration.

Human sexual psychology has in fact evolved in a multitude of directions.[1] Sexuality clearly plays a broad role in human development beyond reproductive concerns. It is a vital element in attachment and relationship bonds, which are crucial in human development. Sexual interests bring people together, helping them past the inherent threat of intimacy with a stranger. They continue to cement the bond, helping them weather relational crises. Sexual subjectivity—being the subject rather than the object of sexual desire—enhances one's sense of self. It is both a profound and primitive way of establishing one's being, one's existence. Sexual interests serve more than these functions however.

Sexuality also has existential and transcendent functions. It provides entry into the world of the ecstatic. It expands the limits of the given and opens the possibilities of the potential. Some would call this a spiritual function. Sexuality is also put into the service of needs for power and domination. Human beings seem to have endlessly varied ways of being sexual, including the cruel, the false, the dissociated, the boring, and the meaningless.

In the animal world homosexuality is pervasive: "In fact, homosexuality is so common in other species—and it occurs in such a variety of circumstances—that human homosexuality is striking not in its prevalence but in its rarity" (Fisher 1992:167). Ethological studies of sexual behavior among animals are focused on other-sex behavior, however, not same-sex (which are considered unimportant?), so we have little information about patterns of homosexual relations among animals. Do they share the typical attraction or attachment tendencies or are they inherently different? I don't know. One thing is clear however: there is no line drawn between homosexual and heterosexual individuals in the animal world. Unlike psychoanalysts, ethologists do not assume fundamental difference here.

While homosexuality and bisexuality (and nongenerative forms of heterosexuality) challenge the idea that sexual behaviors are determined by reproductive concerns, perhaps a degree of all human sexual patterns are "hard-wired" into the organism and follow a general pattern, psychically and somatically. Then again, perhaps not. Homosexual sex may reflect other kinds of sexual interests altogether. Perhaps homosexuality is the prime evidence that both relational bonds and desire for ecstatic experience are fundamental themselves, not founded upon other, covert needs, such as reproduction, and may have evolved independently.

Probably there are some biological givens, differentiating men from women (cf. Symons 1979). Indisputably, there are cultural differences. Representations of male and female sexuality are strikingly different not only in content but even more in clarity. Male sexuality is presented as simple and straightforward: men want sex, usually as much of it as possible; they enjoy it and will go to great lengths to procure it; they are fundamentally nonmonagamous, but can be tamed or shamed into monogamy. Female sexuality is a more complex and confusing arena: women may or may not enjoy sex, and both possibilities carry positive and negative valences. Positively framed, cultural discourse contradicts itself about women as it describes women as lacking desire (that is their virtue) and also as seductive (that is their appeal). Negatively put, women are sexually cold, even "frigid," and yet their sexuality is demanding, even devouring. The preservation of social values rests upon women's innate capacity for chastity, but women also apparently have a potential for promiscuity (a word not applied to men unless they are gay) that is capable of destroying the moral fabric of society. The ambiguity of these images of female sexual desire and the values they are laden with confound individual women's experience of their own sexuality.

A man is assumed to be sexual. To be a woman—does that mean one is sexual or not? In what way? Men are desirous, active, and reluctantly monogamous. Do women want to be sexually active, even aggressive? Does passive sex involve desire? Do women desire monogamy? It is difficult to recognize a woman's own sexual interests against this backdrop.

Because passive images of female sexuality are self-negating and active ones connote dangerous, perhaps even evil or pathological desires, sexual subjectivity as a positive attribute in women has little representation in cultural discourse. Freud was not alone in wondering what women want. Apparently no one knows, not even women themselves. The disordered array of possibilities speaks primarily to the question of whether women do (can) claim sexuality as their own or whether they must know it primarily in relation to another's desires and designs.

The role that cultural representations play in shaping individual, internal representations is most apparent in the sexual realm. The complexity of the picture of women's sexuality argues for an inclusive approach, one that would require psychoanalysis to conceptualize the role of culture in individual development. What is required developmentally for a woman to claim her own sexuality? How do the contradictions and omissions in the cultural discourse interact with psychodynamic development within the family? Ideally, we posit a family in which parents experience their own sexuality subjectively and children may freely identify with their parents (of whatever gender). Children need to feel that their loving and erotic desires are received and supported. But here we run into a double bind. How can mothers participate fully if they themselves lack internal representation of women's sexual wholeness? This is a confounding problem. It suggests the ways in which the ambiguity of women's sexual desires is perpetuated.

The great risk for women, of course, is that their sexuality will be constructed around being an object rather than a subject. The father's resistance to the daughter's identification with him, the mother's discomfort with the daughter's desire for her—these are the blank spaces in our polarized gender arrangements that forbid or ignore cross-gender identities and same-gender desire. If the daughter has difficulty claiming the father's assertion of desire or if her own courtship of her mother is not recognized, she is left to identify only with mother and only as object of father's desire, since that is how mother's desire is constructed. Once again, childhood desires are understood within the family narrative primarily in traditional, heterosexually inscribed oedipal terms.

The consequence for women if their sexuality resides primarily in a sense of attractiveness (or lack thereof) rather than of desire is the passive construction of desire. Their active desires are not seen, mirrored, and approved; they fade into lifelessness or become tainted with a sense of badness. These two alternatives are the essence of cultural representations of female sexuality. The family's failures recapitulate the culture's, and the culture in turn continues to mirror this failure, normalizing, even idealizing it.

The daughter's difficulty in claiming desire as her own may also be compounded by the difficulty of holding a positive representation of her physical body, her sexual body. In Susanna Moore's (1989) lovely novel of a (heterosexual) girl's coming of age, *The Whiteness of Bones*, these problems are wonderfully delineated. At puberty Mamie's beloved Hiroshi, the family gardener, violates her trust by putting his hand down her pants. This is the beginning of knowing herself only as the object of male desire: "She felt as though her body, by some mistake or accident, had passed out of her keeping. I did not have it very long, she thought" (11).

Later, as a young woman, she thinks about her teenage encounters with boys: "The best part, it seemed to her, had been the kissing. The hours and hours, all through the night, that she had spent kissing boys" (101). The passion, the "deep, deep comfort and excitement of those kisses" left her rapt, transcendent. Genital sex is another matter. Mamie describes a girl's transformation in adolescence:

> You start out thinking that your vagina is all right, harmless even, and then something happens when you're about thirteen . . . and it all changes. . . . Suddenly it seems ugly and shameful and not at all harmless. . . . I have even considered it from the point of view of aesthetics. Lily and I used to study sex magazines. Obviously *someone* thinks they're attractive, but isn't it interesting that women themselves don't like their vaginas? . . .

The world wins. Something happens along the way and we become ashamed. (200–201)

Through sexual encounters Mamie tries to love her body again and know her own desires. The struggle continues between her growing subjectivity and what the world imposes:

If she was allowed kissing, what else was she allowed? . . . She had only two choices: if she could figure out what it was that she was permitted, she could take the risk and ask for it, or she could find safety and comfort, and even a kind of rigorous, intellectual pleasure, in having nothing at all. (228)

Mamie's story is the story of female development. Teenage girls not uncommonly endure unwanted sexual approaches, intrusive and disturbing, that confuse their sense of their own desires and possession of their own bodies. They succumb to an objectified self-definition.

The problem is not hopeless; women can and do select fragments of available representations culturally and within the family. They identify where they can, with women or with men, and they desire where they dare, likewise. Some of these identities and desires are of course "deviant" ones and require a willingness to bear the burden of difference. This burden weighs heavily on sexual desire however. It is hardly surprising that sexuality is problematic for so many women.

Questionable Desire(s)

Do many women have a happy, fulfilled sense of their own sexuality? A question impossible to answer, evidence nevertheless suggests that much of sexual activity is male-driven, not female-driven, and consequently that studies of heterosexual behavior tell us more about men's sexual interests and expression than women's. Studies that include lesbian and gay male relationships and behavior may be an exception; however, the subjects of these studies are hardly free from the paradigm of heterosexual male desire and behavior.

A widely respected study reports that lesbians have the least amount of sex, gay men initially have the most, unmarried heterosexual couples follow, but finally that traditionally married heterosexual couples are the only ones who continue to have frequent sex (64 percent, at least once a week) after being together more than ten years (Blumstein and Schwartz 1983:196). Further, in heterosexual relationships the one who initiates sex most of the time is far more likely to be the husband (51 percent) than the wife (12 percent). Right of refusal to have sex is a function of power within a relationship, and a wife must "feel truly strong and secure before she would refuse often" (221).

The obvious question then is whether the women in heterosexual relationships are having more sex than they want, i.e., whether the frequency of sex in heterosexual marriages is a reflection of male desires and power, not female. Ethel Person (1980) raised a related question about sexual differences: "Emphasis on inhibition of female sexuality has almost precluded discussions about the quality of male sexuality, which often seems compulsive in the guise of liberated sexuality" (626). Clinically, I have noticed a striking distinction between lesbian and heterosexual sex: women rarely expect or want another woman to be sexual if she doesn't desire it. Coerced sex is not appealing; it is a turnoff rather than a turn-on. Men sometimes do expect compliance even without desire (and may even find it a turn-on). In therapy men often complain that their wives won't do it, while women complain that their partners don't want to do it.

Another, less obvious, question about the statistical tracking of sexual frequency is whether the same events are being tracked. Analyzing the same study, lesbian writer Marilyn Frye argues that they are not:

> 47% of lesbians in long-term relationships "had sex" once a month or less; while among heterosexual married couples only 15% had sex once a month or less. . . . What long-term heterosexual married couples do more than once a month takes on the average 8 minutes to do. . . . What we do . . . considerably less frequently, takes, on average, considerably more than 8 minutes to

do. . . . The suspicion arises that what 85% of heterosexual married couples are doing more than once a month and what 45% of lesbian couples are doing less than once a month is not the same thing. (1990:307)

Further, she adds:

We have no idea how the individual lesbians surveyed were counting their "sexual acts." But this also raises the questions of how heterosexuals counted *their* sexual acts. By orgasms? By whose orgasms? If the havings of sex by heterosexual married couples did take on the average 8 minutes, my guess is that in a very large number of those cases the women did not experience orgasms. (308)

Anthropologists and human ethologists point out that among primates and within a large number of human societies, a long-term relationship with a continuing sexual interest is uncommon. Life-long monogamy is rare; serial monogamy is the norm, with couples seeking new partners after sexual interest wanes. Infidelity even within serial monogamy is also normative, with both males and females equally active in seeking new partners. Long-term monogamous relationships, however, are usually a product of a strongly patriarchal social system, wherein a double standard of infidelity for men and women prevails. In the diversity of human cultures the most common norm is for couples to stay together (not necessarily sexually faithfully) primarily when the family includes more than two children or the couple has reached middle age (Fisher 1992). Elizabeth Meese reminds us that "the erotic requires endless renewal in order to live up to its name" (Meese and Huss 1995:55)

The pattern of women's sexuality in heterosexual marriages is suspect, I believe, and the picture of women's sexuality apart from men complicated. Several sexual patterns are apparent in lesbian culture. There is of course the "lesbian marriage," not unlike heterosexual marriage, which lasts for a long time with a viable though diminished sexuality. It may include children, extended family, and community visibility, just like its counterpart. This long-term monogamy may become progressively asexual (to preserve its monogamy?).

Contemporary nonsexual relationships are reminiscent of *romantic friendships* or *Boston marriages*, the nineteenth-century names for long-term romantic, but—presumably—asexual, relationships between women (Faderman 1981). Now the guilty secret is the lack of sex, not the indulgence in it. Asexuality is often hidden by couples; they accept it as a problem, partly because it does not mirror heterosexuality. Lesbianism is supposed to be about sex. If there's little sex, are women "lovers?"

Asexual lesbian relationships have entered the communal discourse, sometimes affirmatively, sometimes defensively (Rothblum and Brehony 1993). Women who settle into such attachments may or may not complain about the loss of sexual interest: maybe the relationship still feels good—loving and companionable—and they don't want to part in spite of the loss of sexuality. Is it such a loss? Does it reflect a variation of female sexuality?

Serial monogamy is another common pattern in the lesbian community: relationships that last three to six years and then dissolve as one or both partners seek another. The dissolution is often on sexual grounds: sexual passion has disappeared, they seek it elsewhere. Here are lesbians having plenty of sex, just with a variety of partners over time. Monogamy and sexual faithfulness are valued as long as the relationship lasts; transgressions are emotional betrayals.

Another pattern, more characteristic of younger lesbians, exalts lesbian sex, even nonmonogamy, and seeks out diverse sexual experience (including butch-femme sexuality and sadomasochistically inspired encounters), creating new or reviving old images of what lesbian and female sexual desires are (cf. Nestle 1992; Jay 1995). There may be a generational shift in these patterns: youthful assertions of sexual flamboyance may give way to a middle-age movement toward attachment and companionship.

Even when there is not a lot of intercourse going on, there's plenty of discourse. The sexual dialogue in the lesbian community has heated up, with debates over proper sex—indeed, the role of sex at all. A

growing literature of lesbian erotics filters out through the community, offering new images of lesbian and female sexuality. To engage in
this discourse, I find little help in psychodynamic theory.

Lesbian Sexual Discourse

Psychoanalytic writing on lesbian sexual behavior is sparse and uni-
formly (even naively) derogatory. Some psychoanalysts treat "penis-
in-vagina intercourse" as the definition of sex; they write as if disturbed by the fact that lesbians don't realize they're incapable of having sex since there is no penis involved. Edmund Bergler argued that
lesbian sex is infantile, reflecting fixation at the oral stage, because
lovers engage in cunnilingus and suck on each others' breasts (1957:53).
Masud Khan decreed that lesbian sex involved "excessive use of
mouth, tongue, and hand" (1979:93). Jean-Michel Quinodoz writes
that erotization of the skin is defensive and that fingers and tongues
are a substitute for penises (1989). (What are they when men use them
or when women use them on men?) Joyce McDougall views sex
between lesbians as both a disavowal of "sexual reality" (penis in
vagina intercourse?) and an effort to protect the partner from "the
fantasied attacks that the individual would like to make" upon the
partner (1980:133). Psychoanalysts are unclear whether lesbian acts
represent oral-sadism or anal-sadism, but clear that they are based on
sadistic urges (Socarides 1962). Thus lesbian sex is always primitive and
regressive—but somehow heterosexual sex is not, even engaging in
the same acts.

A patriarchal view of sex requires that a penis be present for sex to
have occurred (Frye 1990). Further, sex is largely a genital experience.
Heterosexuals may engage in other acts than penetration, but these are
foreplay, not sex itself. Teenagers learn early in their sexual careers that
anything short of penetration means they have not really had sex.
Both in lesbian discourse and in heterosexual women's literature other
representations of women's desire and sexual experience emerge.
Sexuality only as genital contact may adequately describe (at least
some) masculine experience, but it is too narrow to suit many

women's. Reminiscent of Mamie in *The Whiteness of Bones*, Anna Livia
tells of this constriction in her own history:

> At sixteen sex happened. Full penetrative heterosexual sex. Dull
> but necessary. Certainly nothing to fantasize over. My fantasies
> were about softness and kissing. . . . "Sex is boring." I wrote on
> the toilet wall at school. It seemed I had given up . . . all-over,
> generalized sensuality for sexual activity focusing almost exclu-
> sively on the genitals. (1995:46–7)

Donna Allegra describes her sense of the erotic this way:

> Depictions of desire in the context of love are what turn me on.
> Who has felt as I have for women? That's what I need to see, and
> want to show, in living color on the page. . . . Too much of the
> erotica/lesbian porn I've read lacks a plane of emotional
> involvement, so I turn the page, bored. I've always felt that the
> sexiest part of a woman was her mind, and it is in my psyche that
> I know desire. (1995:78)

A limited conception of sexuality also appears in much psychoanalytic discourse. Psychoanalysis views lesbian sex (and perhaps
women's desire) as "pregenital." A consultant of mine once referred to
lesbian sex as "breast dependent" to indicate its pregenital quality.
(Surely if any sexuality is organized around preoccupation with
breasts, it is heterosexual male sexuality.) This privileging of certain
sexual behaviors, partners, and interpretations renders lesbians inherently immature. Instead a more diffuse, less genitally focused sexuality
may be truer to "authentic" female desires, i.e., sexuality that is not
male-determined. Some recent psychoanalytic writers have expanded
the definition of the erotic, also grounding it in relationship, especially
in the sensuous physical bond between mother and child (Wrye and
Welles 1994). Happily, the literature by lesbians places lesbian interpretations of their own sexual experience in the center. Some of these
interpretations include translations into psychodynamic concepts.

When lesbian writers addressed the problem of failed desire, they
argued that the tendency of lesbian partners to move toward fusion

eased the necessary tension between self and other that generates sexual desire.[2] Distance and difference fuel sexual desire; familiarity and fusion deprive couples of that tension (cf. Person 1988). This explanation suggests why serial monogamy is the norm in so many cultures. Women are more likely to create such a merger with each other as a consequence of early mother-daughter relationships.

Sexuality with a new person presents one with an Other, allowing one to be both subject and object in the sexual experience. When the other becomes fully a self as well, emotional intimacy is deeper but the erotic draw weaker. As intimacy grows, a sense of family begins, and familial ties are stirred, consciously or unconsciously. When lovers become too much family, sex may feel like incest. Perhaps, given women's early endowment for relatedness, lesbians reach deeper levels of emotional intimacy, and the incestuous feel of sex together is greater. The mother's homophobia, transmitted to the daughter in their early romance, may also be in play here. One author observes that women who are content to be in asexual relationships with each other often have had an "extremely close relationship with a sibling, usually a sister."[3] The greater incidence of women actually being victims of incest may affect long-term sexuality as well.

Other explanations for loss of sexual interest in lesbian relationships over time rely upon the conditions that hinder women's development of a sexual self: sexual abuse, socialization to be sexually passive, lack of experience and comfort with initiating sex, and suppression of aggressiveness in women (Nichols 1987). All women endure at least some of these constraints; a relationship of two women has twice the chance of being burdened here. Internalized homophobia can also prevent women from expressing their sexual interests. All these reasons apply. Short-term relationships and affairs are full of passion. The problem emerges with the longevity of the relationship.

Lesbian writing has moved away from comparing lesbian and heterosexual relationships and toward asserting that lesbian sex has its own norms. One of them might well be a deemphasis on sex. The concept of the intimate, loving romantic friendship or long-term companionship is having a small revival as a viable image for some lesbian relationships. Some writers suggest that women's disorientation from their own sexuality is profound; others suggest that a slighter interest in sex is quite ordinary, "natural," not requiring extended explanations (Rothblum and Brehony 1993; Jay 1995).

In fact, if women set the frequency of sex in most relationships, the data might look very different. Women, at least lesbian women, apparently have little use for nontranscendent sex, sex not fueled by great passion or erotic heat. When initial passion is more or less spent, many don't seem to seek perfunctory orgasms (orgasms not preceded by great arousal and desire) with their partners. Why? Is this fundamentally different from men? Does it reflect lack of sexual subjectivity? Is it different when women masturbate (as many women continue to do even after partner sex has waned), i.e., is masturbation transcendent or does it have a perfunctory feel? Does an active long-term sexuality with the same partner depend upon male drives or even upon strong self-other (subject-object) dynamics?

Psychoanalyst Ethel Person (1980) argues that "gender orders sexuality." She writes:

> There is a wealth of clinical evidence to suggest that, in this culture, genital sexual activity is a prominent feature in the maintenance of masculine gender while it is a variable feature in feminine gender. Thus an impotent man always feels that his masculinity, and not just his sexuality, is threatened. . . . While women may suffer the consequences of sexual inhibition, sexual expression is not critical to personality development. Many women have the capacity to abstain from sex without negative psychological consequences. . . . In men, there is such a rigid link between sexual expression and gender that their sexuality often appears driven rather than liberated. (619–620)

She points out that "any discrepancy between female and male sexuality is viewed as problematic for females" and that male sexuality, emphasizing orgasm and performance "is used as the sexual standard for both sexes" (624). Implicit in her perspective is not only the idea that male and female sexuality may be differently constructed but also that there is much more variation between women than between men.

The other pattern of sexual expression among lesbians reacts against the subordination of sex to attachment, sometimes consciously. Lesbians involved in sexual role-playing—butch and femme or even s/m encounters—also emphasize genital sexuality and power relations. They assert that sexual tension is necessary for sexual heat and that polarized roles heighten the tension and turn up the heat (Nestle 1992).

The creation of butch and femme as cultural identities, first by Havelock Ellis, Krafft-Ebing, and their colleagues and later elaborated on by lesbians themselves, gave women images to contradict the prevailing image of female sexuality as passive or even nonexistent. As Esther Newton (1984) and Lillian Faderman (1991) note, given new language and concepts by sexologists, lesbians were able to explore sexuality in ways not available to their predecessors, not even to women who lived together for a lifetime. The image of the butch entered the public arena, encoding a way for women to express both desires and identities.

During the greatest suppression of homosexuality—the forties through the mid-sixties—butch-femme identity became a social code within working-class lesbian groups (there was little community). Women who wished to participate had to appear as butch or as femme to show they understood the rules, that they were part of the group, not an outsider who might threaten the secrecy of their sexual lives. Middle-class lesbians were often appalled by the appearance of masculinity and exaggerated femininity. The rigidity of these class-gender distinctions mirrored the same in heterosexual culture (Blumstein and Schwartz 1983; Faderman 1991). Again, social imagery determined or influenced individual experience of desire.

Role-playing went underground within feminism, and lesbian-feminist culture offered a new identity—the androgynous, politically aware and politically correct lesbian who wanted egalitarian sexual relationships. It reemerged however in the sexual arena by the eighties and nineties, emphasizing roles as parts to play rather than identities. The "sex wars" of the eighties that began with feminist efforts to combat pornography expanded into debates about the proper kind of sex for women to have with each other (cf. Snitow, Stansell, and Thompson 1983;Vance 1984). One side argued that butch and femme roles were nonegalitarian and that sadomasochistic sex degraded women. Any sexuality based entirely on self-other complementarity (that antidote to merger, to stifled passion) becomes sadomasochistic sex. The intensely felt eroticism of dominance and submission, the fear and danger invoked, the heightened sexual arousal, are the legacy of patriarchal control of women's sexuality. Perhaps it would be better not to be sexual at all, some women argued (cf. Johnson 1990).

On the other hand, advocates of sexual diversity (the "sex-positive" side) argued that these concerns with politically correct behavior led to the death of sexual desire and thus to asexual relationships. Sex is not about equality, they said, but is about tension, power, submission, and dominance—it is about primitive instincts. Some lesbians advocated sadomasochistic encounters and their trappings to enliven sexual experience. Others adapted butch and femme roles for the same purpose (and gender roles are perhaps simply less extreme versions of sadomasochistic roles).

The dialectical relationship between these two positions yielded something of a synthesis such that butch-femme sexuality is generally conceived as more fluid, more egalitarian now. A woman might be both butch and femme, alternately or in combination. The line between the two has blurred: there are "butchy femmes" and "femmy butches." This altered representation of female sexual possibilities, particularly lesbian, has had its appeal. Some have experimented and decided against, some have experimented and decided in favor of these possibilities. (These experiments have also entered the mainstream youth culture of the eighties and nineties, in which distinctions between homosexuality and heterosexuality are more fluid, bisexuality is chic, and the trappings of s/m encounters are fashionable: leather clothing and piercings of body parts, various sexual identities. Clothing ads suggestive of butch-femme roles are routinely featured in mainstream media.)

These sexual experiments have of course not proven to be a solution to sexual waning in long-term relationships; if anything, their high valuing of sexual desire tilts affairs toward nonmonogamy and relationships toward serial monogamy (cf. Hall 1995). They serve another purpose, however: facilitating a more open discourse by women about women's aggressive and receptive desires. They articulate aspects of female sexuality that have been unspoken and spotlight intensely sexual images of women. That is, they begin to alter cultural representations of women's sexuality within the lesbian community and apparently filter into the heterosexual world as well.

Some women argue that this emerging sexual dialectic is a specifically lesbian discourse and that lesbian sexuality is distinct. Both heterosexual and lesbian sexual norms have in various ways attempted to reinforce a difference. Colleen Lamos, paraphrasing Judith Butler, notes that "heterosexuality is performatively constructed through constant, albeit failed, imitations of its own gender and sexual ideals" (1995:103). Throughout the lesbian discourse some have proscribed forms of lesbian sexuality that could be construed as imitative of heterosexuality (such as butch-femme plays or use of dildos) in an effort to affirm lesbianism on its own, particularly egalitarian, ground.

Consider, however, these lines by Pam Parker, a self-identified butch, who writes: "It might be too late for me / maybe only girls growing up now / will be able to act in ways we call butch / without having to know what we know" (1992:368). Her words suggest the impact of changing representations, altering the gender and sexual possibilities for girls without the social estrangement the butch-identified woman bears. Lamos argues that in spite of "the political and social conflicts between them, heterosexuality and homosexuality do not constitute discrete realms of gendered sexual desire"; they they share a "cultural imaginary" (1995:199). Judith Butler points to the "structures of psychic homosexuality within heterosexual relations, and structures of psychic heterosexuality within gay and lesbian sexuality and relationships" (1990a:121). I have argued likewise (Burch 1992); I find relevance in lesbian sexual representations for all female, all human sexuality.

The revived, expanded-upon role of butch usurps the male prerogative of sexual subjectivity, but in a different way. The butch
actively, aggressively desires sex and claims special sexual expertise, but
she claims it in a paradoxical (even traditionally feminine) way: her
pleasure comes through giving another woman pleasure. The femme,
on the other hand, is cognizant of her own desire, and her desire is for
her own pleasure. She actively desires to be "taken." These roles
emphasize different pleasures, transforming their cultural meaning.
Neither desire is about passivity, fear of saying no, need to be taken
care of, acquiring power for lack of it elsewhere—traditional parameters of femininity within heterosexuality. It is not even about attachment, but is a purely erotic need, a need for sex for its own sake. (That
is not to say of course that relationships formed won't also fall within
these emotional parameters.)

Rather than passive, the femme identity is receptive. Female receptivity opens up as something active, a powerful capacity to respond,
"to embrace the world, to open up to the touch of things both material and immaterial . . . a capacity to live inside the body" (Cvetkovich
1995:128). One woman writes,

> I give her my body and all its idiosyncrasies, its details, its curves
> and aromas, its soft and bony landscape, its reachable and un-
> reachable places. What I accept in being femme is not passivity.
> It is active receptivity—passionate curiosity, that hunger insa-
> tiable—for knowledge, for touch, for power received and trans-
> formed . . . I have to become it, live, and charge it with my own
> imagination. (Cassidy 1992:392)

Orgasm can be experienced as a surrender; it can also be experienced
as taking (one's pleasure) and as reaching after, striving for (the ecstatic).

In the new postmodern lesbian discourse butch-femme positions
are seen as a parody of gender itself, pointing to the role-playing at the
heart of any gendered identity (Butler 1990b). They present new gender possibilities, expanding the categories of gender from two to
more. A lesbian butch is not a man; what she represents is something
altogether different. Her gender is an "other" category. (It has its

counterpart in Native American culture, the tradition of the berdache [Blackwood 1986b; Roscoe 1988]). Likewise the femininity of the lesbian femme differs from the heterosexual model. One woman described wearing new boots to work: her male co-workers greeted her with "Oh, new boots—how butch" and her lesbian friends said, "Oh, new boots—how femme" (Istar 1992:381).

At the same time, these roles do mirror and confirm gender difference as the heart of sexual longing (Quimby 1995). Joan Nestle writes, "If the butch deconstructs gender, the femme constructs gender" (1992:16). What about other differences? I have suggested elsewhere that differences in sexual orientation—between the primary lesbian and the more bisexually oriented lesbian—also serve to generate desire and that this difference is often obscured by butch-femme interpretations, which have greater cultural visibility (Burch 1992). Racial differences afford another dimension of attraction, one that has been opposed culturally, especially within heterosexuality, because it also threatens to subvert an established order. This kind of attraction is less submerged now; interracial couples are becoming more common, even among heterosexuals.

Women's Sexuality Accentuated

The sexual patterns of lesbian relationships and the representations of sexuality within the lesbian community suggest a reappraisal of the picture of women's sexual desires. One can analyze roles and identities from an individual etiological perspective: why did this woman identify with masculinity? Why is that one apparently comfortable with an asexual relationship? Why does this woman value passion above all else? When an individual woman asks herself such questions, the analysis has one meaning (perhaps from curiosity, perhaps toward insight and self-acceptance). When analysts (of whatever profession) ask them, it may have another meaning. Regarding homosexuality, psychoanalysis has generally asked these questions with the understanding that homosexuality is problematic and heterosexuality the desirable outcome.[4]

Another perspective is to look at how a minority community alters the face of the majority community, a perspective that undermines the normative bias of the majority view. If the gate is opened and the minority community no longer excluded from the discourse, the discourse changes. Writing about transsexuality, Gayle Rubin says,

> No system of classification can successfully catalogue or explain the infinite vagaries of human diversity. To paraphrase Foucault, no system of thought can ever "tame the wild profusion of existing things." Anomalies will always occur, challenging customary modes of thought without representing any actual threat to health, safety, or community survival. (1992:473)

Challenging customary modes of thought was an essential activity in the early years of psychoanalysis, but in later years many analysts embraced conventional thought regarding relationships and sexual behavior. The lifelong monogamous marriage has been accepted as the hallmark of mature adult partnerships.

Rubin adds, "Human beings are easily upset by exactly those 'existing things' that escape classification, treating such phenomena as dangerous, polluting, and requiring eradication." This kind of response occurs with "deviant" expressions of sexuality and relatedness even when they cause no pain to the individual. Indeed, the pain of deviancy is usually created by the social response rather than the behavior or identity itself. What is the function of deviant labeling but to generate individual anxiety, which reinforces conformity?

Are these new writings on lesbian sexuality useful in establishing viable representations of female sexuality? Do they help women to recognize and claim a clearer sense of their own sexuality? They may. For example, relatively asexual (at least in the genital sense) attachments may suit some women. If some women (lesbian and heterosexual) desire little sex beyond the initial passion of a new love and desire greater emotional intimacy instead, the emergence of a communal understanding that sanctions their experience frees them to affirm it themselves. Esther Rothblum writes: "If sex determines whether two people are in a couple, then sex takes on tremendous symbolic importance aside from sexual pleasure" (Rothblum and Brehony 1993:6). Is this importance legitimate? Some lesbian couples weigh relationships according to this standard, legitimate or not, creating internal stress. As Marny Hall (1993) remarks, "Without any marker of significance in place besides the magically orgasmic, partners can only experience a less sexually exciting relationship as deficient, and overlooking other forms of intimacy, yearn to recapture past glories" (57).

I suggest that several interpretations may be valid. Sometimes these relationships reflect a variation in desire among women. Sometimes they are a temporary adaptation, progressive rather than regressive, to early sexual trauma and/or a transitional retreat from experiences of coerced or pressured sexual encounters. Sometimes they contain and express nongenital forms of female sensuality and sexual expression that carry the same functions as genital sexuality (i.e., pleasure, attachment, self-affirmation). One woman states: "Making love isn't erotic. It's more sensual, emotional. The erotic takes distance. I don't look at my girlfriend and think how erotic she is. Though I might if I saw a photograph of her" (Livia 1995:41). Is this a different kind of sexuality from heterosexuality or male sexuality? Do these relationships break the grip of patriarchal definitions of sexuality for women?

As with any other cultural representation of sexuality, the problem with the fading of sexuality in a relationship is that one's identity may become fixed there: the problem is limitation of the self. Sexual activity may be avoided, undesired, unchosen for various reasons—because intimacy is enough without it or because one has channeled desire and passion elsewhere (into creativity or spirituality) or because of injury through abuse or homophobia. However, surely it is better not to feel that parts of oneself are simply lost.

Lesbians (and other women) are no better off feeling that the norm of lesbian relationships is asexuality than to expect them to mirror male-determined heterosexuality. What happens to one's identity as a sexual person in such a relationship? The risk here is also that of foreclosing the realm of the potential. Better to know oneself as sexual—at least potentially so—even if not actively sexual for a long time. One's sexuality may exist in dreams or fantasies, in masturbation, in imagination, in the expectation that something new may emerge. As Sandy Huss writes, "Of course they're sexually active: they've got a brain" (Meese and Huss 1995:61).

The possibility remains for women to retrieve their sexuality when responsibility for it clearly lies within, not with a partner who has the role of arousing it. This is the point of difficulty for women, of course—the challenge of shifting from object to subject.

Lesbians whose relationships are patterned by serial monogamy rather than long-term commitment are often asserting the value of the erotic, insisting that it is a crucial aspect of their being, equal to the value of attachment. Counterposed to women for whom asexuality is comfortable, they represent the vitality of women's erotic desires. If the evidence of ethology and anthropology are relevant to industrialized culture, the need to refind oneself sexually with a new partner expresses something innate but culturally denied. An assumption that serial relationships indicate immaturity is a cultural bias.

On the other hand, what happens to attachment needs, and the attendant loss, in serial relationships? This dilemma may be unresolvable. And for lesbians, as for heterosexuals, when children become part of the family, then attachment concerns shift. The lesbian community is currently grappling with this problem and, as long as nuclear families are paradigmatic, will experience the same toll on children.

Butch and femme roles establish another alternative, a highly eroticized expression of polarized female desires. If butch and femme are not simply imitative but are alternative genders, they are still polarized and complementary. Qualities that everyone possesses to some degree—being masterful vs. nurturing, confident vs. shy, knowing vs. naive, strong vs. weak, active vs. passive, dominant vs. submissive, aggressive vs. receptive—are divided up and assigned exclusively. However, even if one partner gives pleasure and another takes pleasure, the subversion of the usual sense of passive and active represents these modes in a new way. Butch women speak of "taking" a woman in order to "give" pleasure. The femme "takes" pleasure from her lover by "giving" herself. The giving and taking commingle: there is active passivity and passive activity.

Unlike the masculine paradigm, the butch aggressively seeks her lover's pleasure: her sexual pleasure is the entire focus of their lovemaking. A femme role is the epitome of self-centered pleasure. The butch role is not without its own pleasure, but it is a more vicarious pleasure, oddly not unlike the woman's in the heterosexual paradigm. This confluence of "masculinity" and "femininity" within each role is one way butch and femme plays subvert traditional gender categories.

The confusion of the cultural discourse on women's sexuality may become embodied by women—as fragmented, disjointed, discontinuous identities, various sexual selves corresponding to various representations available. These identities may alternate, some may dominate. Behind the seductress there is the celibate, behind the reluctant partner the woman with intensely erotic fantasies. Relationships tend to fix one in one place or another, and the individual may begin to believe that this is all of who she is. Parts of oneself are avoided in every relationship; sometimes one leaves a relationship to retrieve them. This loss is especially evident in the sexual arena. It is another kind of challenge to retrieve lost parts of oneself within a relationship and to have this recognized by one's partner rather than seek them elsewhere. Relationships that manage this stay interesting. Individuals need to see their own internal possibilities mirrored externally, especially in the sexual arena, where vulnerability and judgment hover.

My understanding of the various expressions of lesbian sexuality is that they do enrich the cultural discourse; they suggest authentic and viable images of the range of women's sexual interests. The experience of lesbians indicates that women have powerful erotic interests as well as strong attachments and that these can be in conflict. One rarely sees the counterpart of a Boston marriage in male relationships. Why? Is attachment weaker or sexual insistence greater? Is active sexuality a defining part of male identity that then becomes threatened if sexuality wanes? (Compulsive sexuality seems to be a greater problem for men and compulsive relationships a greater problem for women.) Men and women might be fundamentally different in some respects, but perhaps it is again a problem of impoverished representations—in this case for deep male attachments.

Sociobiology and anthropology suggest that an actively constructed sexuality is equally strong in both men and women. Humans may carry innate sexual needs, and even nonreproductive sexuality (such as homosexuality or sexuality during pregnancy or after menopause or with birth control) may be under their influence. If they are programmed in—part of one's "deep structure" psychologically—our psychodynamic language has not been able to express these possibilities fully, largely because it is prone to treating variation as deviance and pathology. Because sexuality is more or less a male province in industrialized cultures, because no well-articulated story of women's sexual interests exists, because the mother's sexuality is invisible, and because the mother-daughter romance is subverted, a woman's sexual subjectivity does not flower. She is already, we might say, deflowered.

Lesbian relationships present women with difficulties and opportunities. No longer is a man around to initiate, even insist on, sex. As lesbians begin to understand their sexuality, to come into their own—taking responsibility for their own sexuality and sexual activities—the dialectic between attachment and eroticism is articulated. If the choice is one of longer attachments with reduced sexuality or of shorter relationships with greater sexuality, choice requires knowing oneself. In longer attachments there is a greater need to choose sexual activity for oneself—rekindling it periodically—rather than relying on a partner to arouse it. It is more clearly a personal choice than in heterosexuality, at least as it has traditionally been constructed. (Of course, the heterosexual paradigm is yielding to great pressure from women for sexual and relational equality.) This is the ground of adult development —the growth of subjectivity—when resignation over the conflict between the attachment and eroticism gives way to something new. After all, these women, they've got a brain.

8

Lesbian Families: The Late Edition of the Family Romance

Lesbians, like gay men, are often thought of as without families. As Kath Weston (1991) has reported, many lesbians lose or radically alter ties with families of origin once they come out. New kinship ties created within lesbian and gay culture have little social recognition. Relationships even between lovers usually lack legal standing, and extended networks of "kin"—friends and ex-lovers who become a committed part of each other's lives, who are similar to the extended family in heterosexual terms—have none at all. The only recognized families lesbians may create are those with children. And, as Weston remarks, because lesbians are characterized as nonprocreative, "the image of the lesbian mother is shocking and disconcerting" (168).

Women having babies with each other is quite an anomaly to those who cannot understand how there can be a family with two mothers and no fathers. Lesbian families are the ultimate effrontery to patriarchy: they challenge the necessity of gender roles, women's dependence upon men, and the fundamental structure of the nuclear family. Some gay men are also creating and raising families together, through adoption, surrogacy, or in extended family relationships with women. This evolutionary turn in the story of the family challenges developmental theory, which presupposes that children require traditional family structures for optimal development.

We do not yet know how negatively mainstream culture will react to these challenges or to what degree it will assimilate them. How these new structures shape the families themselves also cannot be fully appreciated yet. There is some evidence, however, that children do very well in these alternative families. For one thing, these children are always wanted children. They are never the unintended product of fleeting passion or accident, as children born to heterosexual couples sometimes are. This chapter considers some of the psychodynamic tasks of shared mothering and of childraising in alternative families. First, however, it is useful to look briefly at what research has already shown.

Quite a lot of research has been undertaken to determine whether children in lesbian families differ from their peers in meaningful ways. Are they gender-deviant, for example? Are they more likely to become gay themselves? Empirical studies say no to these questions. As Suzanne Slater notes, research comparing children of lesbian and heterosexual families "repeatedly find little or no distinction in the children's gender identity, sex role socialization, or personal sexual orientation" (1995:92). Some argue that this is not good news. One writer states, "I am not pleased to discover that my lesbian sisters pose no threat to the perpetuation of patriarchal child-rearing" (quoted in Slater 1995:93). It is surprising, really, to find alternative mothers raising mainstream children. On the other hand, this evidence softens the concerns of those who believe children will suffer a kind of internalized deviancy as a consequence of their parents' differences.

This somewhat puzzling finding of no difference in gender socialization suggests the power of culture to override even the weight of parental influence. It also suggests how mainstream even alternative families become once they carry the responsibilities of child rearing:

> The experience of raising children is a great equalizer, giving the lesbian parents much in common with heterosexual families with similarly aged children. Their lives look strikingly like those of the other mothers they see arriving at the pediatrician's office, attending parents' night at school, ushering their children into Sunday school class, or taking their seat at the school play. The social institutions set up for families with children suddenly hold

great relevance to the parenting lesbian family, and their needs and interests frequently dovetail with those of their parenting heterosexual friends. (Slater 1995:106)

The parents, once on the outskirts of respectability, have moved toward the center themselves and, intentionally or otherwise, have made them seem more "normal" to those who have always lived there. Just as some are offended at lesbians creating families, others are relieved that a common ground of values and interests is imminently visible. Still, conclusions about the nature of children in homosexual families are inherently tentative. Few of these children have reached adulthood, when they may show more diversity than in their early years (especially during the peer-driven years of adolescence).

Researchers have also questioned whether lesbians' children will suffer emotional problems or developmental deficiencies. They have examined social abilities, self-esteem, ego strength, and emotional expressiveness and again found no differences or, in some cases, superior abilities in children of lesbians (Martin 1993; Benkov 1994). There is indeed enough data to answer these questions and lay them aside, at least for a while. What has not been looked at very often, however, are the psychological tasks and psychological consequences of lesbian parenting for the parents. How do women handle the tasks—indeed, what are the tasks?

Lesbians raising children inhabit a social frontier. There are no cultural or historical precedents for families with coequal mothers. There are certainly no role models externally, and the internal worlds of the individual women who live on this frontier probably do not contain any representations of mother and mother with baby. They have had to piece together their own conceptions of how the family would look and feel and how it would even come into being.

Gender Images and Parental Identities

The common assumption in psychodynamic literature that lesbians are inherently gender deviant may be correct to a point, but its corollary is that deviancy is pathological. Many lesbians confront both internalization of the assumption of pathology and uncomfortable internal representations of their own femininity before they can come to parenthood happily. If maternal desires are some kind of hallmark of femininity (and if these are distinct from the desires of men to be parents), then lesbians confront the traditional feminine icon of the Mother in their decision.

Lesbian gender roles, I have argued, are more broadly and more fluidly constructed than traditional femininity (or masculinity), with more options—social, personal, and interpersonal—available. Not all individual lesbians, of course, claim this fluidity or breadth, and some struggle with more rigid or more conflicted feelings and ideas about their gendered self. For one lesbian becoming a mother might be an affirmation of her feminine self, for another it may be confirmation of what was doubtful to her, for another it contains some defiance of femininity—after all, having a child without a man is still an "unfeminine" thing to do—and for another it has nothing at all to do with gender, it simply seems to be a very human thing to do. In other words, how the decision is held may or may not be a reworking of a gendered sense of self.

Although butch and femme are rarely established roles in lesbian relationships, between couples who do identify as butch and femme, according to Weston's research, there is "no pre-ordained correspondence between biological motherhood and their respective gendered identifications" (1991:172). Contrary to a "one-dimensional and inaccurate" portrait of what it means to be butch—a simplistic equation of butch and femme with masculine and feminine—the femme woman is not always the one who gives birth. Her research does not suggest what childbearing means, if anything, in relation to gender for women who do not identify with traditional femininity, but it does make clear that the desire to bear a child exists independently of traditional gender constructions. The internal sense of femininity, masculinity, or androgyny may even be altered in the process of deciding to bear or raise children; it may continue to evolve in the course of child rearing.

Children in lesbian families become aware that their families are different somewhere during their second or third year. This awareness usually takes the form of realizing that they do not have a father in the family (awareness of having a biological father is another matter and sometimes comes later). They may ask for a Daddy, question why there is no Daddy, or even assign one mother (or alternately each mother) a temporary title of Daddy, without much sense of gender roles or implications.

In doing this, children are playing with presence and absence, with possession and nonpossession, with difference and sameness (social difference as well as gender difference) and are not particularly concerned about real or make-believe. This play is not unlike girls claiming to have penises and boys claiming to have vaginas and to produce babies. For example, I watched one two-year-old girl play with the story of the Three Bears, assigning her mothers to be either Mama Bear or Papa Bear while she was Baby Bear. Sometimes she even directed a mom to be Baby Bear, and she elected to be Mama or Papa Bear herself. This child has a clear knowledge of anatomical sex differences, knows she has a vagina and could one day have a baby, knows that boys have penises, but she sometimes also likes to ask if boys can have babies come out of their bodies and seems disappointed to hear again that they can't. In other words, she is a rather typical child working on her understanding of sex differences and of family differences.

If mothers are uncomfortable with being assigned the role of Papa or Daddy, even in play, because their own gendered sense of self has been challenged or because they fear the misunderstanding of extended family or of outsiders, this kind of play will be curtailed.[1] In lesbian families such play has the ability to allow a child to tentatively claim all the possibilities—being both different from and the same as other children simultaneously. It helps the child master difference and also suggests that this family difference is about the parents, not about the child. Such play tends to fall away as reality and make-believe become more sharply divided. (In heterosexual families this play is also likely to be curtailed and gender assignments strictly enforced. I have observed preschoolers with heterosexual parents express a longing to have two mothers after they have played with children from lesbian families. This can, of course, be threatening to their parents.)

Lesbian families may (accurately) have a sense that the world is watching them—their extended families, neighbors, parents of their children's friends, teachers, sometimes even the media. At first they are an anomaly to others, the object of curiosity or hostility. Are they regular parents sharing the usual concerns? When it turns out that for the most part they are, as their presence becomes accepted (and even acceptable), the sense of being object rather than subject diminishes.

During this process, however, gender is again often the focus. Their own sense of being proper mothers or parents is solidifying. All new mothers go through some degree of this other- and self-scrutiny, since mothers are treated as the determining factor in children's lives. Their capacity for nurturing and for empathy, for firmness and good judgment, for patience and understanding, is being weighed. Women who are lesbian may emerge from the early years of parenting with a more clearly defined sense of gendered self, i.e., what they claim for themselves in supposedly gender-linked traits. As they accomplish all the family tasks themselves, the ones that mothers are supposed to fulfill and the ones that fathers are supposed to handle, the relevancy of gender diminishes even further.

In addition to gender identity issues, the other concern of early childhood is the emerging family triangle. The child falls in love with, wants to possess, the parent. But which parent? Both, of course, just as in heterosexual families. Here, however, the story may be rewritten, depending not only on the child but on the mothers as well and how they have conceived or reconceived their own sense of family structure. It is impossible to discuss the family triangle without first considering how lesbians handle the place of two mothers, or of two women, if both are not considered to be coequal mothers.

Family Structures and Parental Dynamics

Heterosexual families vary enormously in the structure of the family. Traditional families leave the majority of the child care to the mother, with father relatively absent. He may be a disciplinarian, an authority figure, or a pal; he may have little function within the family other than working and relaxing. More egalitarian families try to even out the childcare between the parents, but real equality is rarely achieved (Schwartz 1995). Generally the basic responsibility is still held by the mother, and she is clearly the one to whom the child turns for comfort and safety. The father may still be very important as secondary parent, playing with, teaching, and nurturing the child. Some few heterosexual families grant the father a primary role while the mother is more involved in work.

Lesbian families also differ in their structure. How a family aligns itself will depend upon the inner sense of self (internal representation) of each woman as mother or parent. Some women strongly identify with mothering or nurturing and long for children. Other women see themselves as potential mothers or parents without perhaps the intense longing but, nevertheless, with an openness to growing into the role of parent. Others, of course, clearly do not wish to be parents (cf. Ireland 1993).

Like heterosexual families, lesbian parents may evolve into distinct roles based on natural inclination: they do what they like best or feel most able to do in child rearing. Their roles are also determined by economic factors—for example, who works more. Women who have children reluctantly, largely because the partner wants to, may choose a secondary role in the family, allowing the partner clearly to be the mother. They are a member of the family, but not a parent. Their family name reflects this position: the children call them by their first name or by some name other than *Mom*. In other families one partner is considered to be the other parent, but not mother. She is simply the other parent—not mother, not father, not aunt, not any socially recognized (as yet?) position, but nevertheless a parent, very involved, and very important. She may also have a special name within the family or be called by her first name (as the mother may).

The family alignment also depends upon the dynamics of power within the family. If one woman wields more power within the relationship, her needs and desires about whether they will parent as coequals or whether one will take a secondary role may determine the family structure. Power differences are often increased or at least made more visible when partners become parents.

The way the family came into being also influences family structure. If one woman is the biological mother and nursed the baby for an extended period of time, their bond may supersede all other considerations. This is not inevitable, however. There are families in which the nonbiological, non-nursing mother has the primary bond with the child even in the early years and families in which the coequality of the mothers is established very early, with allowances made for the needs of the nursing pair.

Similarly with adoption. If one parent is the official adoptive mother (and in most states this is the only arrangement possible), through the arduous process of adoption she may become primary. Like the biological mother, her position as adoptive parent may have been determined by her greater motivation for being a mother or a sense of self that is more congruent with being Mother. Some states and certain counties within some states allow for same-sex second parent adoption. Whether biological mothers and adoptive mothers encourage or permit their partners to become the other parent legally usually reflects emotional dynamics within the relationship: confidence in or commitment to the relationship, the balance of power between them, and individual internal representations of both self and other as Mother.

The Two-Mother Family

Some families make it past all of the barriers into coequal parenting, establishing themselves as two-mother families. Both are mother, both are called some version of mother (Mommy and Mama, or sometimes a name from another culture that signifies Mother). Within lesbian culture a parent who has no biological tie is easily seen as another parent—like other familial kinds of bonds, many lesbians recognize psychological ties as sometimes equal to, sometimes even superseding, biological ones (cf. Weston 1991). Thus two women may be seen by others within their own community as equal mothers, regardless of whether one of them is the biological parent.

To those outside of lesbian families, this recognition of psychological bonds as primary sometimes initially generates skepticism, confusion, or even negation of a nonbiological parent, as if biological ties are always most significant. When heterosexual couples adopt a child, they sometimes meet a similar resistance (e.g., people may inquire about the "natural" parents), but generally their position as parents is granted both legal and social recognition. Lesbian parents may find it difficult to establish their mothering roles as coequal in a social sense, especially if a second-parent adoption does not take place. Thus they lack the usual social mirrors that help heterosexual parents to assume their parental identities.

Lesbians who are coequal mothers often focus their relationship on finding equality of position within the family, especially in the children's early years when each is finding her way. They may have different roles or tasks, but they try to equalize the valence of each role. Neither claims exclusive right to be the primary parent. Between them they conceive the family of mother and mother and child, at times in conflict with their own initial desires or inclinations.

How do they become two mothers psychologically? At heart, it's a tough role to share. Sharing the work of mothering is relatively easy— it's so demanding, all mothers could have another one there to help. Sharing the role though—the place of mother—is another matter. The mother-child bond may tolerate other children, but does it tolerate another mother? Culturally, we make room for two grandmothers, each having a special, even equal, place, but we have no conception of two mothers. Developmental psychology is shaped by the premise that there's one mother and she is primary, no matter how involved a father is. The role of father has never been conceived or constructed as primary. Even when a man is the primary parent, there is not another primary parent as well (except in the case of gay male couples). After all, primary means primary. There can't be two.

If neither woman is interested in being secondary, however, she must make psychological room for another mother without feeling diminished as mother herself. Does it disrupt something deep and internal? Perhaps. There is a period of adjustment. In therapy one woman described her experience this way: "It took me maybe a year for this process to feel complete. It happened because I kept feeling and behaving like Jacob's mother, no matter how much Julie did too. We raced each other to the crib when Jacob cried. I knew I was Jacob's mother and felt Jacob knew it too. Julie knew she was too and felt the same. We all just knew." It's a curious and challenging paradox—claiming something as absolutely your own—the role of mother—and simultaneously sharing it. Women who wish to be comothers must develop the space for this internally as they evolve into a family.

The period of adjustment to coequal mothering may take considerable time. One mother may rush over when the baby cries and take him or her out of the other mother's arms. It seems right because she feels like the mother. One may constantly interrupt when her partner feeds, changes, bathes the baby. Each has the mother instinct, the sense that she knows "her" baby best. It takes time for one mother to allow the other, with her own impulses and her own knowledge of the baby, to take her place not only with the baby but in her own internal psychological diagram of the family.

This shift in the mothers' internal world is meaningful for their own development. Their inner representations of self and other are being modified; their capacity to contain two distinct maternal images grows. These images alter, even transform, their understanding of a mothering person as they observe each other in different capacities as mother. Sometimes these alterations will be therapeutic, allowing, for example, a more nurturing sense of mother or a more effectual sense of mother to develop. The process may also further each woman's sense of differentiated self within relationship as she incorporates their differentness as mothers and observes the child as different from both. Archaic images of mother and child and their bond are shifting.

Another paradox within this triangle of mother and mother and baby is the oneness both mother-baby pairs may feel with each other. Does the undifferentiated state of "primary maternal preoccupation" (Winnicott's [1956] term) occur between the baby and both mothers? I believe it often does. Both mothers may experience their own state of oneness with the baby, which gradually gives way to a more differentiated state as development progresses. Does the baby in turn experience herself as part of both, or are the two initially variations on the same mothering person/function to her? Possibly the latter. One new mother described this sense of herself and her partner as merged in the baby's perception this way: "Sometimes we joke about whether we are the two-headed mother to her." At the same time, the baby seems to distinguish mothers clearly, sometimes preferring one, sometimes the other. The facility with which children seem able to exist within this paradox recalls Daniel Stern's (1985) research into early infant states. He finds that children do live in concurrent states of differentiation and oneness with the parents.

The demands of this task for mothers are great. Each developmental phase of the child requires negotiation of a new balance, since each phase requires different skills from the parents and one may excel where the other struggles. What do they do when the child alters the balance of power by preferring one over the other—treating one as primary parent? If they wish to maintain their coequality, they may try to equalize things again by considering whether the child is acting out something latent within their parental relationship. For example, if one mother lacks confidence in herself or the other, if one is having difficulty sharing the role of mother, or if one is withdrawing defensively through her own fears of being rejected as mother, they may air these fears and eventually find their balance again. On the other hand, children typically will prefer one or the other at times. Can they allow the child to exercise her/his preferences without being too threatened? Can they accept and communicate behaviorally to the child that this is not destructive and that no one is irreparably hurt or disappears when this happens? These are the tasks for them to master.

Confidence in one's partner, some convergence of values about childcare, and ability to support each other through the inevitably stressful times of parenting are necessary if they are to respect each other's position as coequal mother. Like all families, lesbians have periods of success and periods of failure in managing the demands of family life. The balance of their joint positions as mothers is always in the background. For example, during stressful periods one or both may fantasize that she is the "real" mother (psychologically) and may even imagine her partner disappearing. The trials of managing triadic relationships are perhaps different in this way than in heterosexual families where the woman is granted exclusive rights to be primary parent; jealousy and competitiveness still occur, of course, but may be given a different meaning.

At the same time, in lesbian families there are special rewards in a three-party relationship. Each has a partner who is as preoccupied with this baby as she is, someone who is happy to center her life around the baby, happy to talk about or listen to every new event, to discuss the anxieties, to hold the baby psychologically, willing to bear full responsibility, as she does. This shared position is the strength of lesbian parenting, one that I believe is an asset to both mothers and child.

Having a third party in the relationship changes the dynamics of the couple. Again, this change occurs in all families but may be manifested differently in lesbian relationships. When the two-ness of a lesbian couple becomes an intense oneness—the pull toward merger—sometimes one or both will seek three-ness (perhaps reflecting the value of a "third" in the archaic mother-daughter relationship). Having a triangle at home can serve this function well, opening things up. One woman expressed it this way, "We've both fallen in love, but with the same person. We are extremely close in our love for Lily. It's a triangle that works in all directions." This is a fine example of the fluidity with which states of merger may alternate, even perhaps coexist, with a distinct sense of self. This idyllic solution, however, may itself become stressful in the period of triadic relationships.

Sometimes couples fail to develop the balance they need; the family structure becomes skewed in favor of one woman as mother, against the other's desires. This unwanted asymmetry may also be determined by the child. Some argue that children require one primary attachment figure for optimal growth, that attachment needs are innately structured toward a primary figure. Perhaps this is true of some children. The presence—and success—of coequal lesbian families does challenge this assumption however. Perhaps it is not an essential need, but a socially constructed one. The ability to form several attachments may give a child an adaptive advantage, and indeed some children are quite flexible, capable of diverse attachments of great significance. Some form strong attachments not only to parents but to extended family as well—who may be friends rather than blood relatives (Weston 1991).

Asymmetry within the family isn't necessarily problematic. If everyone finds a place more or less congruent with inner representations of self and other, an asymmetrical balance works well. However, if asymmetry is treated as if it is determined by the child, when it is actually determined by one or both parents, it is stressful and creates internal conflicts for the child. If the individual women cannot ultimately share the position of Mother, an uneasy compromise may be reached, one that never leaves either of them quite settled in the family. Preexisting differences in power are exacerbated, and what was tolerable before the child may no longer be tolerable. The partners may separate.

Children who do appear to have coequal ties—these ties are obviously inferred—form deep attachments to both mothers that may alternate in temporary cycles of favoring one over the other, handling a need for a "primary" attachment figure (if there is such a need) by temporarily choosing one and excluding the other. This triangulated dynamic overlaps with the so-called oedipal period. I have argued that the Oedipus myth is a poor analog for female development. In lesbian families it clearly becomes irrelevant as gender is not the crucial factor, although jealousy, competitiveness, and triangulated desires still appear. I refer to this developmental period as the period of triadic relations, even though some triangulation is present from birth unless there is only one parent.

The Family Triad

The psychological task of the family triad, as traditionally constructed, is to solidify the child's erotic desires toward the opposite sex and identification with her or his same-sex parent. Benjamin (1988) has argued that this traditional construction, enacted within the family, becomes pathological for both boys and girls. When children are unable to identify with their opposite-sex parent, much is foreclosed for them that can be refound only in complementary heterosexual relationships structured on the terms of dominance and submission. Boys and girls are both at risk of holding the feminine in contempt. I have argued that there is a similarly devastating loss for girls when their erotic/romantic desires for the mother are unseen or rejected within the family.

In traditional psychoanalytic theory the role of father has been to serve as a third, opening up the mother-child dyad and allowing the child to have more psychological separateness from the mother. With daughters, it is assumed that the father's gender allows a new kind of relatedness, one of desire rather than identification. The father is Other and can therefore be desired; his otherness also facilitates individuation and differentiation. With sons, the father's gender allows a new kind of identification, based on gender, which also helps the boy to differentiate himself from the mother. He can then desire her as Other.

Following this paradigm, one would conclude that sons of lesbians would be impaired in their gender identity, having no father to identify with, and daughters might be impaired in their separation-individuation, having no father to desire. Research specifically directed to these premises has shown that this is not the case (Steckel 1985). Given this empirical evidence, psychoanalytic developmental theory needs revision. Apparently gender and gender differences are not as salient as other factors in separation-individuation processes. Children seem to be capable of sorting out their socially determined gender assignments in other ways. Girls handle differentiation from the mother without the presence of an other-gendered parent to desire. Again, gender's place of importance in psychoanalytic theory is suspect.

Family triangles, of whatever gender, are emotionally complicated, and heterosexual families often rely upon received cultural "truths" to guide them through the difficulties. The father's position as outsider is inscribed by the culture, suggesting that he and the mother not question it. Indeed, one of the great political and social struggles of contemporary American culture is the question of the father's place in the family: conservatives demand that fathers' return to their traditional places and (at least some) liberals debate why.

Children identify (or try to) with their parents, of whatever gender, and they tend to fall in love with them, i.e., love them passionately, as well. The wounds to the child come when these feelings are rejected or negated; the child then tries to mold herself/himself into other more acceptable emotional positions. Some of the problems of gender-polarized families may be relieved by families with two mothers, where alignments are not presumed to fall along prescribed paths and may be allowed to fall where they may.

Children in lesbian families may be passionate about both mothers—equally, differently, temporarily, or fixedly. The same is true in heterosexual families, but when homophobia threatens the parental response to same-sex desires, it will be channeled into some other route, negated, rejected, or humiliated. These childhood love affairs are important for development but don't seem to determine later sexual orientation as irrevocably as predicted by traditional theory. Other factors, both innately determined and socially constructed, must be quite influential as well. Parental anxieties, which make them try to channel a child's desires in the "proper" direction, are understood as rejection by the child. Rather than the beneficial effect society assumes it to be, such parental concern is problematic.

Children are busy trying to solve the problem of how to have both parents and of mastering existence within a three-party relationship. Competition with the same-sex parent is traditionally seen as the hallmark of this period in parent-child relationships. While competition with either parent marks stages in the struggle when mastery is difficult, it is not the defining state of any of the relationships during this time. I believe it is the salient dynamic only when mastery has failed altogether—usually because the parents, not the child, have been unable to master their roles. When parents cannot respond freely or when they cannot allow the child's own feelings to unfold freely, competition emerges as a way of managing the dilemma. The child needs responsive assistance from parents; she does not need to be required to love or desire one at the expense of the other. She must come to realize that the parents love each other in a way that excludes her to a degree and that generational differences are significant. But she also knows that each of them loves her in a way that sometimes excludes the other.

The child learns that triangular relationships are complex, sometimes paradoxical, and must involve different roles—all parties are not the same here. She also learns that dyadic relationships are fundamental, even within a triangular structure, and that space for a third position of some kind keeps the dyad psychologically viable rather than constricting. In other words, this developmental period is not only about coming to terms with impossibility, as it has traditionally been constructed, but also about discovering and confirming the possibilities that do exist. If all goes well, she can carry this knowledge into her future family relationships with partner and child.

A family in which both parents are women may be well suited to this task of managing love triangles without permanently excluding anyone. Girls often do not replace their romantic bond with the mother when they turn to the father—they want both. I have suggested that the story of Demeter and Persephone describes the girl's early development far better than the Oedipus story. The girl's early development is organized less around competition and conquest and more around maintaining complex dual relationships. Women's skill in managing relationships derives from this early task and relationships often become a lifelong concern. As parents in a lesbian family, they can draw upon this early mastery to balance the desires and threats that emerge here. The period of triadic relations within their new families will replay their own archaic experience.

Psychodynamic theory tends to look at this period of triangulated relationships in terms of the challenges that face the child. It is important for us to recognize the challenges facing the parents as well. Their own feelings of jealousy and competition are aroused by the triangle. Everyone has her time on the outside. Each has to allow herself to be chosen and not chosen. Each has to maintain her position of importance in the family and not retreat defensively. These are the same challenges that face heterosexual families, but to preserve the familiar lines of heterosexual construction parents may make greater efforts to control the outcome and use defensive retreats from uncomfortable homosexual feelings within the family triad. Their designated roles also tend to place fathers off-center in the family drama.

Some people question how the child will sort out having two mothers, how the child will manage triadic relations without traditional roles in place. I suggest that it is less of a problem for the child than for the parents. If the parents work out their own struggles well, the child's feelings and interests may fall into place relatively easily (as easily, that is, as in any other kind of family). The challenge for children lies in dealing with the stigma of deviancy assigned to their family by the culture, not with any internal deficit within the family. As in heterosexual families, the parents' conflicts over the child's emerging development are the difficulty, not fixed needs of the child that would require a particular kind of family structure.

Lesbian families challenge stereotypes and cultural truisms both about lesbians and about good families. The idea that lesbians and gay men are not inclined toward family life and children is giving way to an awareness that many homosexuals are becoming parents. Psychology and psychoanalysis have played an influential role in establishing these stereotypes. The influence of lesbian and gay clinicians and theorists (and like-minded heterosexual ones) is being felt within traditional disciplines and will perhaps (one can only hope) lead the field to repair some of the damage it has done. There are many opportunities for creative research in this area.

Lesbian and gay families show that family roles are not inherently gender-linked, that mothers can "father" and that fathers can "mother." They challenge deeply embedded beliefs that children must have one primary caretaker and that this must be a mother. They challenge some psychoanalytic assertions about differences in mothers and fathers and their roles in the family. The viability and health of lesbian families disputes the idea that children need parents of both genders for proper development. Perhaps they will ultimately challenge the belief that children must be socialized into polarized gender roles.

Notes

Introduction: Other Women

1. I used this example of Freud's misreading in my first book *On Intimate Terms* as well. To readers of my first book I apologize for this redundancy, but I find it so enlightening about the developmental course of psychoanalytic theory that I have used it again. Freud's attempt to make a radical divergence from his own culture in understanding sexuality was obviously limited in ways he never saw. He apparently never realized that he had misread this passage from Plato.

2. Some of these cultures are described in Blackwood, *Anthropology and Homosexual Behavior*; Stoller, *Observing the Erotic Imagination*; Roscoe, *Living the Spirit* and *The Zuni Man-Woman*.

3. Each clinical account is a composite of two or more individuals in order to protect the identity of everyone involved. Details and events are altered, but the underlying clinical experience remains as true to the experience as possible.

1. The Mythology of the Family Romance

1. The degree to which a child is concerned with the father is surely a consequence of the degree to which the father is an involved caretaker.

2. For forty years various types of studies have found no difference here. For example, see Armon, "Some Personality Variables"; Gartrell, "The Lesbian as a 'Single' Woman"; Weis and Dain, "Ego Development"; Wolfson, "Toward the Further Understanding of Homosexual Women."

3. In her biography, *Anna Freud*, Elizabeth Young-Bruehl argues that they were not, but she offers no evidence. How could she?

4. The term continues to have some currency. Cf. Faderman, *Surpassing the Love of Men* and *Odd Girls*, as well as Rothblum and Brehony, *Boston Marriages*.

2. Family Romances and Sexual Solutions

1. Cf. Stoller, *Observing the Erotic Imagination*, and Chodorow, "Heterosexuality as a Compromise Formation," for a recent critique of this position.

3. Gender Identities, Lesbianism, and Potential Space

1. Caldwell and Peplau, "The Balance of Power"; Lynch and Reilly, "Role Relationships"; Marecek, Finn, and Cardell, "Gender Roles"; and Peplau, Padesky, and Hamilton, "Satisfaction in Lesbian Relationships," all show this as an important value in lesbian relationships.

2. Cf. Allen, *The Sacred Hoop*; Blackwood, "Sexuality and Gender"; and Roscoe, *The Zuni Man-Woman*.

4. Mothers and Daughters in the Family Romance

1. The major works representing a feminist psychodynamic approach to women's development—Chodorow, *The Reproduction of Mothering*; Benjamin, *The Bonds of Love*; Gilligan, *In a Different Voice*; and Jordan et al., *Women's Growth in Connection*—have this neglect in common.

2. Cf. Bernstein, "Gender-Specific Dangers"; Blum, "The Concept of Erotized Transference"; Kumin, "Erotic Horror"; and Person, "The Erotic Transference in Women and Men."

5. Themes in Lesbian Relationships: The Question of Merger

1. Some of these studies include Peplau et al., "Loving Women"; Tanner, *The Lesbian Couple*; Peplau, Padesky, and Hamilton, "Satisfaction in Lesbian Relationships"; Blumstein and Schwartz, *American Couples*; Caldwell and Peplau, "The Balance of Power"; Kurdek and Schmitt, "Partner Homogamy"; Murphy, "Lesbian Couples and Their Parents"; Eldridge and Gilbert, "Correlates."

2. Several studies of these historical relationships are especially important for the continuity they provide to understanding contemporary views of lesbians as well: Smith-Rosenberg, "The Female World of Love and Ritual"; Katz, *Gay American History*; Rich, "Compulsory Heterosexuality"; Faderman, *Surpassing the Love of Men*.

3. Peplau et al. "Loving Women"; Peplau, Padesky, and Hamilton, "Satisfaction in Lesbian Relationships"; Blumstein and Schwartz, *American*

Couples; Eldridge and Gilbert, "Correlates," all point to this in one way or another.

4. In addition to my own papers, upon which this chapter has drawn, Krestan and Bepko, "The Problem of Fusion"; Kaufman, Harrison, and Hyde, "Distancing for Intimacy"; Roth, "Psychotherapy with Lesbian Couples"; Elise, "Lesbian Couples," have also argued this.

6. Themes in Lesbian Relationships: The Balance of Power

1. Several studies of lesbian relationships point to this desire for equality: Peplau et al, "Loving Women"; Tanner, *The Lesbian Couple*; Blumstein and Schwartz, *American Couples*; Schneider, "The Relationships of Cohabiting Couples."

2. Marecek, Finn, and Cardell, "Gender Roles"; Lynch and Reilly, "Role Relationships"; Caldwell and Peplau, "The Balance of Power"; Schneider, "The Relationships of Cohabiting Couples."

7. Lesbian Sexuality/Female Sexuality: Searching for Sexual Subjectivity

1. One can imagine how this diverse evolution is itself adaptive. Now, as humans have increased survival rates from childbirth and lowered infant mortality rates, as overpopulation has become a greater threat than underpopulation, nonreproductive sexuality may be highly adaptive.

2. Several of my own early papers, which in revision have been used in chapter 5 of this book, fall into this category. See note 4 in that chapter for other examples.

3. Esther Rothblum, in Rothblum and Brehony, *Boston Marriages*, p. 11, makes this observation. She does not draw the same implication from this that I do, i.e., the threat of sex feeling incestuous in such relationships dampens their fervor.

4. In *The Psychology of Women* Helene Deutsch provides an excellent example of this attitude. After acknowledging that she helped an unhappy woman become happy in a lesbian relationship, she adds that, nevertheless, this is "far below what psychoanalysis demands of an adult personality."

8. Lesbian Families: The Late Edition of the Family Romance

1. In a 1993 custody case in Virginia in which a child was removed from his lesbian mothers, the judge cited as evidence of disturbance the fact that this not quite three-year-old had sometimes called one of his mothers Daddy.

References

Allegra, Donna. 1995. "Between the Sheets: My Sex Life in Literature." In Karla Jay, ed., *Lesbian Erotics*. New York: New York University Press.

Allen, Paula Gunn. 1986. *The Sacred Hoop.* Boston: Beacon.

Armon, Virginia. 1960. "Some Personality Variables in Overt Female Homosexuality." *Journal of Projective Techniques* 24:293–309.

Balmary, Marie. 1982. *Psychoanalyzing Psychoanalysis.* Baltimore: Johns Hopkins University Press.

Batten, Mary. 1992. *Sexual Strategies.* New York: Tarcher/Putnam.

Becker, Carol. 1988. *Unbroken Ties: Lesbian Ex-Lovers.* Boston: Alyson.

Bell, Alan, and Martin Weinberg. 1978. *Homosexualities: A Study of Diversity Among Men and Women.* New York: Simon and Schuster.

Benjamin, Jessica. 1988. *The Bonds of Love.* New York: Pantheon.

Benkov, Laura. 1994. *Reinventing the Family.* New York: Crown.

Bergler, Edmund. 1957. *Homosexuality: Disease or Way of Life?* New York: Hill and Wang.

Bergmann, Martin. 1980. "On the Intrapsychic Function of Falling in Love." *Psychoanalytic Quarterly* 49:56–77.

Bernstein, Doris. 1991. "Gender-Specific Dangers of the Female Dyad in Treatment." *Psychoanalytic Review* 78:37–48.

Berzoff, Joan. 1989. "Fusion and Heterosexual Women's Friendships: Implications for Expanding Our Adult Developmental Theories," *Women and Therapy* 8:93–107.

Blackwood, Evelyn. 1984. "Sexuality and Gender in Certain Native American Tribes: The Case of Cross-Gender Females." *Signs* 10:27–42.

— 1986a. *Anthropology and Homosexual Behavior.* New York: Haworth.

— 1986b. "Breaking the Mirror: The Construction of Lesbianism and the Anthropological Discourse on Homosexuality." In Evelyn Blackwood, ed., *Anthropology and Homosexual Behavior,* pp. 1–17. New York: Haworth.

Blum, Harold. 1973. "The Concept of Erotized Transference." *Journal of the American Psychoanalytic Association* 21:61–76.

Blumstein, Philip, and Pepper Schwartz. 1983. *American Couples.* New York: Morrow.

Bristow, A. R., and P. L. Pearn. 1984. "Comments on Krieger's 'Lesbian Identity and Community: Recent Social Science Literature.' " *Signs* 9(4):729–732.

Burch, Beverly. 1985. "Another Perspective on Merger in Lesbian Couples." In Lynne Bravo Rosewater and Lenore Walker., eds. *A Handbook of Feminist Therapy.* New York: Springer.

— 1986. *Psychotherapy and the Dynamics of Merger in Lesbian Couples.* In Carol Cohen and Terry Stein, eds. *Psychotherapy with Gay Men and Lesbians.* New York: Plenum.

— 1992. *On Intimate Terms: The Psychology of Difference in Lesbian Relationships.* Urbana, Ill.: University of Illinois Press.

— In press. "Erotic Transference Beween Women in Psychotherapy: A Perspective on Female Development." *Psychoanalytic Psychology.*

Butler, Judith. 1990a. *Gender Trouble: Feminism and the Subversion of Identity.* New York: Routledge.

— 1990b. "Gender Trouble, Feminist Theory, and Psychoanalytic Discourse." In Linda Nicholson, ed., *Feminism/Postmodernism,* pp. 324–340. New York: Routledge.

Caldwell, Mayta, and Letitia Anne Peplau. 1984. "The Balance of Power in Lesbian Relationships." *Sex Roles* 10:587–599.

Caplan, Paula. 1981. *Barriers Between Women.* New York: Spectrum.

Cass, Vivian. 1979. "Homosexual Identity Formation: A Theoretical Model." *Journal of Homosexuality* 4(3):219–235.

— 1984. "Homosexual Identity: A Concept in Need of Definition." *Journal of Homosexuality* 9:105–126.

Cassidy, Christine. 1992. "Walt Whitman: Model Femme." In Joan Nestle, ed. *The Persistent Desire.* Boston: Alyson.

Chodorow, Nancy. 1978. *The Reproduction of Mothering.* Berkeley and Los Angeles: University of California Press.

— 1992. "Heterosexuality as a Compromise Formation: Reflections on the Psychoanalytic Theory of Sexual Development." *Psychoanalysis and Contemporary Thought* 15:267–304.

— 1994. *Femininities, Masculinities, Sexualities*. Lexington: University of Kentucky Press.

Crisp, Polly. 1988. "Projective Identification: Clarification in Relation to Object Choice." *Psychoanalytic Psychology* 5(4):389–402.

Cvetkovich, Anne. 1995. "Recasting Receptivity: Femme Sexualities." In Karla Jay, ed., *Lesbian Erotics*. New York: New York University Press.

Davis, Madeline, and David Wallbridge. 1981. *Boundary and Space: An Introduction to the Work of D. W. Winnicott*. New York: Bruner/Mazel.

Deutsch, Helene. 1944. *The Psychology of Women*. New York: Grune and Stratton.

Dimen, Muriel. 1991. "Deconstrucing Difference: Gender, Splitting, and Transitional Space." *Psychoanalytic Dialogues* 1:335–352.

Dinnerstein, Dorothy. 1976. *The Mermaid and the Minotaur: Sexual Arrangements and Human Malaise*. New York: Harper and Row.

Downing, Christine. 1989. *Myths and Mysteries of Same-Sex Love*. New York: Crossroad.

Eldridge, Natalie, and Lucia Gilbert. 1990. "Correlates of Relationship Satisfaction in Lesbian Couples." *Psychology of Women Quarterly* 14:43–62.

Elise, Dianne. 1986. "Lesbian Couples: The Implications of Sex Differences in Separation-Individuation." *Psychotherapy* 23:305–310.

Ellis, Havelock. 1928. "Sexual Inversion." In *Studies in the Psychology of Sex*, vol. 2. Philadelphia: Davis.

Faderman, Lillian. 1981. *Surpassing the Love of Men: Romantic Friendship and Love between Women from the Renaissance to the Present*. New York: Morrow.

— 1991. *Odd Girls and Twilight Lovers*. New York: Columbia University Press.

Fairbairn, W. R. D. 1986. *Psychoanalytic Studies of the Personality*. London: Routledge and Kegan Paul.

Fast, Irene. 1990. "Aspects of Early Gender Development: Toward a Reformulation." *Psychoanalytic Psychology*, supplement. 7:105–117.

Fisher, Helen. 1992. *Anatomy of Love*. New York: Fawcett Columbine.

Flax, Jane. 1978. "The Conflict Between Nurturance and Autonomy in Mother-Daughter Relationships and Within Feminism," *Feminist Studies* 4:171–189.

— 1990. *Thinking Fragments*. Berkeley: University of California Press.

Freud, Sigmund. 1905. "Three Essays on the Theory of Sexuality." In James Strachey, ed., *Standard Edition of the Complete Psychological Works of Sigmund Freud* [*SE*], 7:125–243. 24 vols. 1953–1974. London: Hogarth.

— 1920. "The Psychogenesis of a Case of Homosexuality in a Woman." *SE,* 18:145–172.

— 1923. "The Infantile Genital Organization." *SE,* 19.

— 1925. "Some Psychical Consequences of the Anatomical Distinction Between the Sexes." *SE,* 19.

— 1931. "Female Sexuality." *SE,* 21:221–243.

Frye, Marilyn. 1990. "Lesbian 'Sex.' " In Jeffner Allen, ed., *Lesbian Philosophies and Cultures*. Albany: New York: SUNY Press.

Gagnon, John, and William Simon. 1973. *Sexual Conduct: The Social Sources of Human Sexuality*. Chicago: Aldine.

Gay, Peter. 1988. *Freud: A Life for Our Time*. New York: Norton.

Gartrell, Nanette. 1981. "The Lesbian as a 'Single' Woman." *American Journal of Psychotherapy* 34:502–510.

Gilligan, Carol. 1982. *In a Different Voice*. Cambridge: Harvard University Press.

Golden, Carla. 1987. "Diversity and Variability in Women's Sexual Identities." In Boston Lesbian Psychology Collective, eds., *Lesbian Psychologies*. Urbana: University of Illinois Press.

Goldner, Virginia. 1991. "Toward a Critical Relational Theory of Gender." *Psychoanalytic Dialogues* 1:249–272.

Hall, Marny. 1993. " 'Why Limit Me to Ecstasy?' Toward a Positive Model of Genital Incidentalism Among Friends and Other Lovers." In Esther Rothblum and Kathleen Brehony, eds., *Boston Marriages: Romantic but Asexual Relationships Among Contemporary Lesbians*. Amherst: University of Massachusetts Press.

— 1995. "Not Tonight, Dear, I'm Deconstructing a Headache: Confessions of a Lesbian Sex Therapist." In Karla Jay, ed., *Lesbian Erotics*. New York: New York University Press.

Hamilton, Edith. 1969. *Mythology*. New York: Mentor.

Hancock, Emily. 1981. "Women's Development in Adult Life." *Dissertation Abstracts International*, 42, 2504 B University Microfilms, 81–25, 484.

Harris, Adrienne. 1991. "Gender as Contradiction." *Psychoanalytic Dialogues* 1:197–224.

Hertzberg, Max. 1962. *Myths and Their Meaning*. Boston: Allyn and Bacon.

Horney, Karen. 1926. "The Flight from Womanhood: The Masculinity Complex in Women." *International Journal of Psychoanalysis* 7:325–336.

Ireland, Mardy. 1993. *Reconceiving Women: Separating Motherhood from Female Identity*. New York: Guilford.

Isay, Richard. 1989. *Being Homosexual*. New York: Farrar, Strauss, and Giroux.

Istar, Arlene. 1992. "Femme Dyke." In Joan Nestle, ed., *The Persistent Desire*. Boston: Alyson.

Jay, Karla, ed. 1995. *Lesbian Erotics*. New York: New York University Press.

Jay, Karla, and Allen Young. 1977. *The Gay Report: Lesbians and Gay Men Speak Out About Sexual Experiences and Lifestyles*. New York: Summit.

Johnson, Miriam. 1975. "Fathers, Mothers, and Sex Typing." *Sociological Inquiry* 45(1):15–26.

Johnson, Sonia. 1990. *The Ship That Sailed Into the Room*. Estancia, N.M.: Wildfire.

Jones, Randall, and John DeCecco. 1982. "The Femininity and Masculinity of Partners in Heterosexual and Homosexual Relationships." *Journal of Homosexuality* 8:37–44.

Jordan, Judith, Alexandra Kaplan, Jean Baker Miller, Irene Stiver, and Janet Surrey. 1991. *Women's Growth in Connection*. New York: Guilford.

Jowett, Benjamin. 1933. *The Works of Plato*. New York: Tudor.

Katz, Jonathan. 1976. *Gay American History*. New York: Harper and Row.

Kaufman, Phyllis, Elizabeth Harrison, and Mary Lou Hyde. 1984. "Distancing for Intimacy in Lesbian Relationships." *American Journal of Psychiatry* 141:530–533.

Khan, Masud. 1979. *Alienation in Perversion*. New York: International Universities Press.

Kinsey, Alfred, Ward Pomeroy, C. Martin, and Paul Gebhard. 1953. *Sexual Behavior in the Human Female*. Philadelphia: Saunders.

Klein, Melanie. 1928. "Early Stages of the Oedipus Complex." In *Love, Guilt, and Reparation, and Other Works: 1921–1945*. New York: Free.

Knight, Robert. 1940. "Introjection, Projection, and Identification." *Psychoanalytic Quarterly* 9:334–341.

Krafft-Ebing, Richard von. [1886] 1965. *Psychopathia Sexualis*. New York: Stein and Day.

Krestan, Joanne, and Claudia Bepko. 1980. "The Problem of Fusion in the Lesbian Relationship." *Family Process* 19(3):277–289.

Krieger, Susan. 1983. *The Mirror Dance: Identity in a Woman's Community*. Philadelphia: Temple University Press.

Kumin, Ivri. 1985. "Erotic Horror: Desire and Resistance in the Psychoanalytic Situation." *International Journal of Psycho-Analytic Psychotherapy* 11:3–20.

Kurdek, Lawrence A., and J. Patrick Schmitt. 1987. "Partner Homogamy in Married Heterosexual Cohabiting, Gay, and Lesbian Couples." *Journal of Sex Research* 23(2):212–232.

Lamos, Colleen. 1995. "Taking on the Phallus." In Karla Jay, ed., *Lesbian Erotics*. New York: New York University Press.

LaTorre, Ronald, and Kristina Wendenburg. 1983. "Psychological Characteristics of Bisexual, Heterosexual, and Homosexual Women." In M.W. Ross, ed., *Homosexuality and Social Sex Roles*, pp. 123–145. New York: Haworth.

Leonard, Marjorie. 1966. "Fathers and Daughters: The Significance of 'Fathering' in the Psychosexual Development of the Girl." *International Journal of Psycho-Analysis* 47:325–334.

Lester, Eva. 1985. "The Female Analyst and the Erotized Transference." *International Journal of Psycho-Analysis* 66:283–293.

Lewes, Kenneth. 1988. *The Psychoanalytic Theory of Male Homosexuality*. New York: Simon and Schuster.

Livia, Anna. 1995. "Tongues or Fingers." In Karla Jay, ed., *Lesbian Erotics*. New York: New York University Press.

Loulan, Joanne. 1988. "Research on the Sex Practices of 1,566 Lesbians and the Clinical Applications." *Women and Therapy* 7(2–3):221–234.

Lynch, Jean, and Mary Ellen Reilly. 1985/1986. "Role Relationships: Lesbian Perspectives." *Journal of Homosexuality* 12:53–69.

McDougall, Joyce. 1980. *Plea for a Measure of Abnormality*. New York: International Universities Press.

— 1986. "Eve's Reflection: On the Homosexual Components of Female Sexuality." In Helen Meyers, ed., *Between Analyst and Patient: New Dimensions in Countertransference and Transference,* pp. 213–228. New York: Analytic.

— 1989. "The Dead Father: On Early Psychic Trauma and Its Relation to Disturbance in Sexual Identity and Creative Activity." *International Journal of Psycho-Analysis* 70:205–219.

Magee, Maggie, and Diane Miller. 1992. "She Foreswore Her Womanhood: Psychoanalytic Views of Female Homosexuality." *Clinical Social Work Journal* 20:67–88.

Mahler, Margaret, Fred Pine, and Anni Bergman. 1975. *The Psychological Birth of the Human Infant*. New York: Basic.

Marecek, Jeanne, Stephen Finn, and Mona Cardell. 1982. "Gender Roles in the Relationships of Lesbians and Gay Men." *Journal of Homosexuality* 8:45–50.

Martin, April. 1993. *The Lesbian and Gay Parenting Handbook*. New York: Harper.

Meese, Elizabeth, and Sandy Huss. 1995. "Staging the Erotic." In Karla Jay, ed. *Lesbian Erotics*. New York: New York University Press.

Mencher, Julie. 1990. "Intimacy in Lesbian Relationships: A Critical Re-examination of Fusion." *Works in Progress*. Wellesley, Mass.: Stone Center for Developmental Services and Studies.

Miller, Jean Baker. 1976. *Toward a New Psychology of Women*. Boston: Beacon.

Mitchell, Valory. 1988. "Using Kohut's Self Psychology in Work with Lesbian Couples." *Women and Therapy* 8(1/2):157–166.

Moore, Susanna. 1989. *The Whiteness of Bones*. New York: Penguin.

Morton, Susan. 1993. *Sexual Identity and Sexual Object Choice: An Object Relations Theory Description of Development*. Berkeley: Wright Institute.

Murphy, Bianca Cody. 1989. "Lesbian Couples and Their Parents: The Effects of Perceived Parental Attitudes on the Couple." *Journal of Counseling and Development* 68(1):46–51.

Murstein, Bernard. 1976. *Who Will Marry Whom? Theories and Research in Marital Choice*. New York: Springer.

Nestle, Joan. 1992. *The Persistent Desire*. Boston: Alyson.

Newton, Esther. 1984. "The Mythic Mannish Lesbian: Radclyffe Hall and the New Woman." In Martin Duberman, Martha Vicinus, and George Chauncey, eds. *Hidden from History: Reclaiming the Gay and Lesbian Past*. New York: New American Library.

Nichols, Margaret. 1987. "Lesbian Sexuality: Issues and Developing Theory." In Boston Lesbian Psychology Collective, eds., *Lesbian Psychologies*. Urbana: University of Illinois Press.

O'Connor, Noreen, and Joanna Ryan. 1993. *Wild Desires and Mistaken Identities*. New York: Columbia University Press.

Ogden, Thomas. 1987. "The Transitional Oedipal Relationship in Female Development." *International Journal of Psycho-Analysis*, 68:485–498.

— 1989. *The Primitive Edge of Experience*. Northvale, N.J.: Aronson.

Oldham, Sue, Doug Farnil, and Ian Ball. 1982. "Sex Role Identity of Female Homosexuals." *Journal of Homosexuality* 8:41–46.

Ortner, Sherry, and Harriet Whitehead. 1984. *Sexual Meanings: The Cultural Construction of Gender and Sexuality*. Cambridge: Cambridge University Press.

Parker, Pam. 1992. "The Long View." In Joan Nestle, ed., *The Persistent Desire*. Boston: Alyson.

Peplau, Letitia Anne. 1981. "What Homosexuals Want in Relationships." *Psychology Today*, March 1981, pp. 28–38.

Peplau, Letitia Anne, Susan Cochran, Karen Rook, and Christine Padeskey. 1978. "Loving Women: Attachment and Autonomy in Lesbian Relationships." *Journal of Social Issues* 34 (3):7–27.

Peplau, Letitia Anne, Christine Padesky, and Mykol Hamilton. 1982. "Satisfaction in Lesbian Relationships." *Journal of Homosexuality* 8:23–35.

Person, Ethel Spector. 1980. "Sexuality as the Mainstay of Identity: Psychoanalytic Perspectives." *Signs: Journal of Women in Culture and Society* 5(4):605–630.

—— 1985. "The Erotic Transference in Women and Men: Differences and Consequences." *Journal of the American Academy of Psychoanalysis* 13:159–180.

—— 1988. *Dreams of Love and Fateful Encounters: The Power of Romantic Passion.* New York: Norton.

Ponse, Barbara. 1978. *Identities in the Lesbian World.* Westport, Conn.: Greenwood.

Quimby, Karen. 1995. "She Must Be Seeing Things *Differently.*" In Karla Jay, ed., *Lesbian Erotics.* New York: New York University Press.

Quinodoz, Jean-Michel. 1989. "Female Homosexual Patients in Psychoanalysis." *International Journal of Psychoanalysis* 70:55–63.

Raymond, Janice. 1986. *A Passion for Friends: Toward a Philosophy of Female Affection.* Boston: Beacon.

Rich, Adrienne. 1980. "Compulsory Heterosexuality and Lesbian Experience." *Signs* 5:631–660.

Richardson, Diane. 1984. "The Dilemma of Essentiality in Homosexual Theory." *Journal of Homosexuality* 9:79–90.

Roscoe, Will. 1988. *Living the Spirit.* New York: St. Martin's.

—— 1991. *The Zuni Man-Woman.* Albuquerque: University of New Mexico Press.

Ross, Nathaniel. 1975. "Affect as Cognition: With Observations on the Meanings of Mystical States." *International Review of Psychoanalysis* 2:79–93.

Roth, Sallyann. 1985. "Psychotherapy with Lesbian Couples: Individual Issues, Female Socialization, and the Social Context." *Journal of Marital and Family Therapy* 11:273–286.

Rothblum, Esther, and Kathleen Brehony. 1993. *Boston Marriages: Romantic but Asexual Relationships Between Women Among Contemporary Lesbians.* Amherst: University of Massachusetts Press.

Rubin, Gayle. 1992. "On Catamites and Kings: Reflections on Butch, Gender, and Boundaries." In Joan Nestle, ed., *The Persistent Desire.* Boston: Alyson.

Schneider, Margaret. 1986. "The Relationships of Cohabiting Lesbian and Heterosexual Couples: A Comparison." *Psychology of Women Quarterly* 10:234–239.

Schwartz, Adria. 1986. "Some Notes on the Development of Female Gender Role Identity." In Judith Alpert, ed., *Psychoanalysis and Women: Contemporary Reappraisals*, pp. 57–89. Hillsdale, N.J.: Analytic.

Schwartz, Pepper. 1995. *Love Between Equals.* New York: Simon and Schuster.

Shavelson, Eileen, Mary K. Biaggio, Herb Cross, and Robert Lehman. 1980. "Lesbian Women's Perceptions of Their Parent-Child Relationships." *Journal of Homosexuality* 5:205–215.

Silverman, Doris. 1987. "What Are Little Girls Made Of?" *Psychoanalytic Psychology* 4:315–334.

Slater, Suzanne. 1995. *The Lesbian Family Life Cycle.* New York: Free.

Smith-Rosenberg, Carroll. 1975. "The Female World of Love and Ritual: Relations Between Women in Nineteenth-Century America." *Signs* 1(1):1–30.

Snitow, Ann, Christine Stansell, and Sharon Thompson. 1983. *Powers of Desire: The Politics of Sexuality.* New York: Monthly Review.

Socarides, Charles. 1962. "The Historical Development of Theoretical and Clinical Concepts of Overt Female Homosexuality." *Journal of the American Psychoanalytic Association* 11:386–412.

—— 1968. *The Overt Homosexual.* New York: Grune and Stratton.

—— 1981. "Psychoanalytic Perspectives on Female Homosexuality." *American Journal of Psychotherapy* 34:510–515.

Spence, Donald. 1982. *Narrative Truth and Historical Truth.* New York: Norton.

Stanley, Julia P., and Susan Wolfe. 1980. *The Coming Out Stories.* Watertown, Mass.: Persephone.

Steckel, Ailsa. 1985. "Separation and Individuation in Children of Lesbian Parents." Ph.D. diss., Wright Institute, Berkeley.

Stern, Daniel. 1985. *The Interpersonal World of the Infant.* New York: Basic.

Stoller, Robert. 1985. *Observing the Erotic Imagination.* New Haven: Yale University Press.

Symons, Donald. 1979. *The Evolution of Human Sexuality.* New York: Oxford University Press.

Tanner, Donna. 1978. *The Lesbian Couple*. Lexington, Mass.: Heath.

Tyson, Phyllis. 1982. "A Developmental Line of Gender Identity, Gender Role, and Choice of Object Love." *Journal of the American Psychoanalytic Association* 30:61–86.

Vance, Carole. 1984. *Pleasure and Danger: Exploring Female Sexuality*. Boston: Routledge and Kegan Paul.

Vetere, Vivian. 1982. "The Role of Friendship in the Development and Maintenance of Lesbian Love Relationships." *Journal of Homosexuality* 8(2):51–62.

Weis, Charles, and Robert Dain. 1979. "Ego Development and Sex Attitudes in Heterosexual and Homosexual Men and Women." *Archives of Sexual Behavior* 8:341–356.

Weston, Kath. 1991. *Families We Choose*. New York: Columbia University Press.

Wilson, Elizabeth. 1984. "Forbidden Love." *Feminist Studies* 10:213–226.

Winnicott, D. W. 1956. "Primary Maternal Preoccupation." In *Through Paediatrics to Psycho-Analysis*. New York: Basic, 1975.

—— 1965. *The Maturational Processes and the Facilitating Environment*. New York: International Universities Press.

—— 1971. *Playing and Reality*. London: Tavistock.

Wolfson, Abby. 1984. "Toward the Further Understanding of Homosexual Women." *Journal of the American Psychoanalytic Association* 35:165–173.

Wrye, Harriet, and Judith Welles. 1994. *The Narration of Desire: Erotic Transferences and Countertransferences*. Hillsdale, N.J.: Analytic.

Young-Breuhl, Elisabeth. 1988. *Anna Freud*. New York: Summit.

Index

Between Men ~ Between Women
Lesbian and Gay Studies
Lillian Faderman and Larry Gross, Editors

Edward Alwood, *Straight News: Gays, Lesbians, and the News Media*

Corinne E. Blackmer and Patricia Juliana Smith, editors, *En Travesti: Women, Gender Subversion, Opera*

Alan Bray, *Homosexuality in Renaissance England*

Joseph Bristow, *Effeminate England: Homoerotic Writing After 1885*

Claudia Card, *Lesbian Choices*

Joseph Carrier, *De Los Otros: Intimacy and Homosexuality Among Mexican Men*

Terry Carter, *Noël Coward and Radclyffe Hall: Kindred Spirits*

John Clum, *Acting Gay: Male Homosexuality in Modern Drama*

Gary David Comstock, *Violence Against Lesbians and Gay Men*

Laura Doan, editor, *The Lesbian Postmodern*

Allen Ellenzweig, *The Homoerotic Photograph: Male Images from Durieu/Delacroix to Mapplethorpe*

Lillian Faderman, *Odd Girls and Twilight Lovers: A History of Lesbian Life in Twentieth-Century America*

Linda D. Garnets and Douglas C. Kimmel, editors, *Psychological Perspectives on Lesbian and Gay Male Experiences*

Richard D. Mohr, *Gays/Justice: A Study of Ethics, Society, and Law*

Sally Munt, editor, *New Lesbian Criticism: Literary and Cultural Readings*

Timothy F. Murphy and Suzanne Poirier, editors, *Writing AIDS: Gay Literature, Language, and Analysis*

Noreen O'Connor and Joanna Ryan, *Wild Desires and Mistaken Identities: Lesbianism and Psychoanalysis*

Don Paulson with Roger Simpson, *An Evening in the Garden of Allah: A Gay Cabaret in Seattle*

Judith Roof, *Come as You Are: Sexuality and Narrative*

Judith Roof, *A Lure of Knowledge: Lesbian Sexuality and Theory*

Claudia Schoppmann, *Days of Masquerade: Life Stories of Lesbians During the Third Reich*

James T. Sears and Walter L. Williams, editors, *Overcoming Heterosexism and Homophobia: Strategies That Work*

Alan Sinfield, *The Wilde Century: Effeminacy, Oscar Wilde, and the Queer Moment*

Jane Snyder, *Lesbian Desire in the Lyrics of Sappho*

Chris Straayer, *Deviant Eyes, Deviant Bodies: Sexual Re-Orientations in Film and Video*

Ruth Vanita, *Sappho and the Virgin Mary: Same-Sex Love and the English Literary Imagination*

Thomas Waugh, *Hard to Imagine: Gay Male Eroticism in Photography and Film from Their Beginnings to Stonewall*

Kath Weston, *Families We Choose: Lesbians, Gays, Kinship*

Kath Weston, *Render Me, Gender Me: Lesbians Talk Sex, Class, Color, Nation, Studmuffins...*

Carter Wilson, *Hidden in the Blood: A Personal Investigation of AIDS in the Yucatán*